the
DIY *Wedding*

the DIY *Wedding*
Celebrate Your Day
Your Way

by Kelly Bare

Foreword by Natalie Zee Drieu

CHRONICLE BOOKS
SAN FRANCISCO

Library of Congress Cataloging-in-Publication Data:
Bare, Kelly.
    The DIY wedding : celebrate your day your way / By Kelly Bare.
        p. cm.
    ISBN-13: 978-0-8118-5784-0
    1. Handicraft. 2. Wedding decorations. 3. Wedding costume. I. Title.
    TT149.B363 2008
    745.594'1—dc22

                        2006035206

Manufactured in China
Designed by Mary Beth Fiorentino

Distributed in Canada by Raincoast Books
9050 Shaughnessy Street
Vancouver, British Columbia V6P 6E5

10 9 8 7 6 5 4 3 2 1

Chronicle Books LLC
680 Second Street
San Francisco, California 94107

www.chroniclebooks.com

This book is dedicated to my husband,
Jonathan Cohen, and to Nancy Bare and
Lynn Cohen, two indispensable "Ys"
in our own DIY wedding.

CONTENTS

FOREWORD	**8**
INTRODUCTION	**10**
Chapter One **GETTING STARTED**	**14**
Get Organized	15
Get Inspired	30
Get Moving	33
Deep Breath: Pat Yourself on the Back	37
Chapter Two **ATTIRE**	**38**
Here Comes the Dress	40
Complete the Package	54
The Groom's Outfit	63
The Bridesmaids' Ensembles	66
Deep Breath: Relax, Gorgeous	73
Chapter Three **INVITATIONS** **(and Other Ways to Spread the Word)**	**74**
Keep It Simple	76
Invitation Options	80
Easy Save-the-Dates	91
The Wedding Web Site	94
Deep Breath: Signed, Sealed, Delivered	95
Chapter Four **PHOTOS AND VIDEO**	**96**
DIY Photography	98
DIY Video	106
Deep Breath: Freeze Frame	107
Chapter Five **FOOD AND DRINK**	**108**
DIY Food	109
A Piece of Cake?	116

The DIY Bar...118

Setting the Table....................................123

Deep Breath: Eat, Drink, and Be Married............125

Chapter Six **FLOWERS**   **126**

Flower Basics 127

Hand Flowers..138

Corsages and Boutonnieres..........................142

Centerpieces 144

Deep Breath: Nature's Way..........................147

Chapter Seven **FAVORS**   **148**

Edible Favors 150

Useful/Dual Purpose Favors.........................157

Intangible Gifts 160

Deep Breath: Do Yourself a Favor...................161

Chapter Eight **RINGS**   **162**

Have Your Rings Made...............................163

Rings with a Past..................................167

Deep Breath: All That Glitters 173

Chapter Nine **THE CEREMONY**   **174**

Finding an Officiant...............................176

Make-Your-Own Minister.............................180

Writing Your Own Ceremony and/or Vows 183

Ceremony Music 188

Decorate the Ceremony Space 192

Deep Breath: You Do 193

Chapter Ten **THE RECEPTION**   **194**

Decorate the Reception Space 196

Reception Music 202

Deep Breath: It's All Coming Together 209

Chapter Eleven **P.S. CRAFTILY EVER AFTER**   **210**

The DIY Guide..................................212

DIY Rules Recap 213

Contracts 101 214

DIY Team Assignments 216

Resources 218

INDEX   **226**

ACKNOWLEDGMENTS   **228**

FOREWORD

A few days after Christmas in 2005, my then-boyfriend, Gilles, and I were in Paris, ready to spend a few quality days together before I met his family for the first time. On our second night, Gilles had planned a romantic dinner–boat ride along the Seine. It was there, after dinner, that he popped the big question. Suddenly, we were engaged!

My vision for our wedding was one that celebrated our international backgrounds; Gilles is French and I am Chinese American. We settled on a theme of 1930s Paris and Shanghai because we love the style of that era and it fit our cultures so well. Easy, right? Not so. For the first couple months of our engagement, family and friends suggested I meet with "wedding people." Here I became exposed to the commercial pitfalls of wedding planners, florists, caterers, and more. To these professionals, it didn't matter that I had more than ten years' experience in the design world as a creative director. And never mind the fact that I'm a pretty savvy crafter whose job at the time was to help launch the magazine CRAFT. Duh! I can help! But to them, they were the professionals and I was just a big dollar sign.

"Oh sweetie, you are never going to find a location in your budget for an October wedding in the city. Get married next year. Trust me, I've been doing this for 25 years." Translation? "Pay me $6,000 and I will find you something!" Another one said, "Rose balls! I see rose balls hanging down from the fireplace!" Translation? "I did this same thing for the last 20 weddings and it will be easiest for me to do."

Eventually, I took control like I wanted to from the beginning. We had a team of amazing friends and family who lent their creative genius to make our event even more special. Using flowers we bought wholesale, my mother and her friends created striking Japanese ikebana floral arrangements for the ceremony and reception. Custom jewels designed by my friend Kris Nations matched my silk sheath Monique Luhillier wedding dress (which was only $1,500 at Glamour Closet in San Francisco). My girlfriend's mom, Harriette Shakes, and I worked closely to come up with a design for our save-the-dates, invitations, signage, and place cards. I learned about paper and the importance of weight (the heavier it is, the more postage you need!). In the end, the design process was the one I enjoyed most. I learned more than I ever could have if I went with cookie-cutter cards from a stationery store.

Under the pressure of launching CRAFT, I hired a wedding coordinator, Michelle Martinez (www.allureconsulting.com), for partial planning and coordinating "week of" wedding events. (Partial planning fees should be less than $3,500.) Michelle's day-of schedule and lists were a lifesaver: She kept tabs on our families, the wedding party, all the vendor deliveries, and us (because, trust me, I was in no state to keep tabs on myself). Most important, she kept things on schedule. Gilles and I ended up having the wedding of our dreams because we chose the details that meant the most to us, not the default décor that everyone else had.

And that's what you can have with The DIY Wedding as your guide. It blasts a breath of fresh air into the commercial, cheesy world of wedding planning. I would have saved months of headache and money if I had this book when I was engaged! Kelly's insight and advice are so clear. She carefully places all the right steps in order to help you tackle every aspect of your wedding without getting overwhelmed. She also gives you the assurance you need with encouraging reminders, such as my favorite, "DIY doesn't mean you need to do it all yourself"—one of the key nuggets of wisdom I could have used early on.

Thank you, Kelly, for helping us DIYers reclaim the modern wedding!

Natalie Zee Drieu
Associate Editor, CRAFT
Web Editor, Craftzine.com

INTRODUCTION

You're engaged? Congratulations! It's thrilling to find someone to share your life with, and equally thrilling (if not a bit scary) to step into the realm of the *fiancée,* with its many formerly forbidden delights: you get to wear a ring on the fourth finger of your left hand, you get to replace your hand-me-down furniture and mismatched dishes with "real" things, and, yes, *you get to plan a wedding*—your long-awaited, once-in-a-lifetime (knock on wood), let's-make-it-magic wedding. Now, since you're reading this book, may I presume that you're considering Doing It Yourself?

If so, congratulations again. DIY is more than just a snappy acronym—it's a savvy approach to wedding planning, with benefits on many fronts. It saves money by helping you avoid (or work around) wedding vendors and package deals. It's easier on your conscience, because you can control your event's impact on the environment, and you know who's doing the labor. (That'd be you.) It helps you really connect to the spirit of the event, so that when the big day arrives it feels like a rite of passage, a great party, *and* a significant accomplishment all rolled into one. (Naturally, when your guests gush, you can take the credit.) Best of all, a DIY wedding is absolutely your own—and much more beautiful and meaningful than the glitziest straight-from-the-pages-of-a-magazine event, because it's infused with your spirit, your spouse-to-be's, and those of the people you love.

So dig in. This book is a blueprint for making your day turn out your way. It's a step-by-step guide to thinking outside the robin's-egg-blue wedding-industry box and planning a freethinking, fun-loving, completely unique wedding day that reflects your personalities, saves money, and minimizes stress. It offers you inspiration and ideas, as well as simple start-to-finish projects. (Trust me: if the instructions are in here, it's easy.) I'll show you how to budget, plan, and locate all the resources you need to create the event you want. I'll walk you through everything you want to know, from finding unique rings, getting everyone dressed, and creating a thoughtful ceremony to doing up the reception with flowers, favors, and food.

At every step of the planning process, this book puts the necessary inspiration, resourcefulness, and savvy negotiating skills within your reach—no matter who you are. And that's an important point: a DIY wedding is *not* the sole province of the super-crafty. Nor does it have to be kitschy or "homespun." If the phrase "DIY wedding" evokes visions of bridesmaids in patchwork aprons and favors made out of popsicle sticks, think again—a DIY wedding doesn't mean ticky-tacky, and it doesn't mean sacrificing elegance, etiquette, beauty, or polish. But it isn't a perfect affair, either. It won't be a mass-produced, cookie-cutter event. What it *will* be is uniquely you. The DIY wedding is about handmade accents, personal touches, and showing your guests who you (and your soon-to-be-spouse) are.

But don't worry—you certainly don't have to make every last little thing yourself. In fact, where weddings are concerned, "DIY" is a bit of a misnomer. A wedding isn't painting the den, or rewiring a lamp. So it's really more like DIYCEPEWLY ("Do It Yourself, with the Creativity, Effort, and Patience of Everyone Who Loves You"), or, alternatively, DYDTDEY ("Don't You Dare Try to Do Everything

Yourself"). In short, DIY really stands for "Do It Your*selves*"—a group that includes not only your mate but also your family and friends. Remember, a wedding is an awesome, transformative, big-deal life event. As the star of the show, you'll have much more on your mind than place cards when the big weekend rolls around. I know, because I got married not very long ago myself. It was a true DIY wedding, and, in the final countdown, I leaned heavily on family and friends. Their help was invaluable. Instead of running around like a maniac, I was able to get ready, get in the right headspace to walk down the aisle, and then relax and have fun. Trust me: brave DIYers need extra support systems. This book will help you set them up.

I'll also help you decide which jobs only you can do. Throughout the book, I'll help you make sure that the tasks you decide to tackle are projects you really want to do yourself. I urge you to be choosy—to spend your own time and energy on the things that will bring you the most pleasure and make the wedding-planning process as meaningful as possible. You can then apply a broader definition of the DIY spirit elsewhere, turning to friends, family, and other resources you might not realize you have at your disposal. (And for situations where you want to, or have to, use traditional wedding vendors, I'll explain how you can keep the DIY spirit alive by adopting an "à la carte" mantra: *Reject the package. Ask for alternatives. Do it your way.*)

The secret to pulling off *any* big project is to find talented people, delegate, and then let go. If you find yourself getting in over your head, turn to the "Deep Breath" sections at the end of each chapter to regain perspective, then steady your footing and forge ahead. After all, it's your marriage that's most important here, though the wedding industry might beg to differ. Planning a wedding, whether big or small, fancy or casual, is *never* easy, and it doesn't get any easier when you encounter people at every turn who are trying to sell you things you don't really need.

So I urge you to simplify. To take the ceremony more seriously, and the reception less so. To pause now and then in the midst of planning and consider whether you might be getting *just a teensy bit carried away*. (It happens to everybody.) Most of all, I urge you to perpetually ask yourself whether you *really* need to buy something new, or whether something you already own, or could borrow, might work just as well. Begin the decision-making process by assessing what you have on hand—and remember that each choice you make sets the stage for the choices that follow.

Start with a beautiful space. It's a whole lot easier to create a gorgeous wedding against a gorgeous backdrop: Great light. Lush greenery. A stretch of sand. Wide-open skies. Then add great music, delicious (but not necessarily fancy) food, and fun people, and you have the four cornerstones of a terrific event that you can't screw up—no matter how hard you try.

Which is good, because as anyone who's had a DIY itch knows, not everything turns out quite the way you envisioned it would. And could something as monumental as a wedding ever really go off *exactly* as planned? But one thing's for certain: with a little DIY spirit, it can be even more beautiful than you imagined.

One Quick Caveat: The English language has its limitations, such as those pesky gender-specific pronouns. So, for simplicity's sake, I've assumed that you, the recently engaged reader of this book, are female. Taking even more liberties, I've assumed that you're a female bride planning to wed a male groom. But of course I know that same-sex couples want to have DIY weddings, too—and I hope you can and will, with Uncle Sam's full blessing.

GETTING STARTED

CHAPTER ONE

Quick—how long have you been imagining your wedding day? Even if you got engaged yesterday, chances are you've already got a few ideas to work with, and one or two (or twenty) wishes regarding the look and feel of the big event. Let's not forget that you're not marrying yourself—and your spouse-to-be will have ideas and wishes as well. And don't leave out those friends and relations. (It's the rare bride and groom who don't get a healthy dose of input from well-meaning friends and family.) So when you're ready to start planning, the trick is to sift through all the fabulous, maddening, endless, schizophrenia-inducing possibilities and zero in on how to build a wedding that's absolutely right for you. In short, it's time to Get Organized, which will help you Get Inspired, so you can bite the bullet and Get Moving.

Get Organized

First things first: the most crucial piece of the DIY wedding-planning puzzle is figuring out what your resources are—monetary and otherwise—and how to allocate them. You can break the process into three distinct—but interdependent—chunks: set your budget, set your priorities, and set your team. How? Read on.

Set Your Budget

You've heard the jaw-dropping numbers: According to the most recent study by the Fairchild Bridal Group, the average cost of a wedding, *not* including big-ticket items like the engagement ring and the honeymoon, is above the $26,000 mark and climbing steadily. According to www.TheWeddingReport.com, it's more than $27,000. And everybody's cashing in: wedding photography and videography are more than 100 percent more expensive now than they were in 1999, music costs are up by almost 70 percent, and flowers are up by almost 50 percent.

The good news is that a DIY approach and conscious spending—including avoiding those wedding-specific vendors whose prices are skyrocketing—can help stem the rising tide and make the cost of the "average" wedding look ridiculously inflated. The trick is threefold: forget you ever heard those scary figures, set a budget that makes sense for *you,* and then consistently come in *under* it. Because here's the worst news: nearly 50 percent of engaged couples wind up spending more than they originally budgeted.

How can you avoid the pain of blowing your budget? First, be realistic when you build it. Though each wedding budget is unique, based on the bride's and groom's priorities and existing talent pool (here's that interdependency thing I mentioned; more on both those topics in a moment), www.TheKnot.com offers a good rough guide to the biggest-ticket items: reception expenses, including food and liquor, could account for up to 50 percent of your total cost, and attire, flowers, music, and photography could gobble up around 10 percent each. (I also highly recommend The Knot's budgeting tool—it's free, thorough, and easy to use.)

But, of course, *there are no absolutes,* especially with a DIY wedding. One of the main principles of a smart, efficient DIY wedding—the very best kind—is that money spent and energy expended are inversely proportional. (See Figure A.)

Here's an example: You decide to go ahead and pony up for that gorgeous ready-to-wear dress you can't get out of your head, thus freeing up multiple Saturday afternoons you would have spent trying to replicate it—searching for the perfect fabric, finding a seamstress, going to endless fittings. Presto—now you've got time to make your invitations and programs by hand, at little cost. Or, say your sister bakes like Julia Child *and* has a knack for doing flowers. Each task is equally time-consuming, but cake ingredients are readily available and cost very little, whereas nice flowers require some intrepid shopping and a moderately significant investment. So put your sister on oven duty, and pay someone else to do the flowers. In other words, you should only spend big when you don't want to DIY, and, conversely, make sure that your DIY projects have minimal associated costs. It's actually a good illustration of the "time is money" adage.

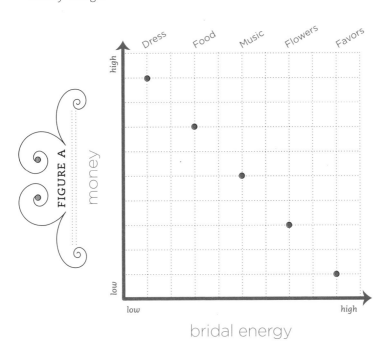

FIGURE A

This whole book is designed to save you money, so I won't belabor the point, but here are some additional helpful hints:

✻ When you're just getting started, for a lark, go to www.costof wedding.com and enter the zip codes of all the venues you're considering. I can't say it's scientific, but it is entertaining—and it may give you a ballpark estimate of the cost difference between a wedding in a big city and one in a small town, or even the difference between weddings held in different neighborhoods in the same city.

✻ When determining how much money you have to work with, approach all possible investors (parents, grandparents, long-lost uncles, sugar daddies) separately. Politely ask what they might be comfortable contributing, if anything. Asking this question may be awkward, but chances are they know it's coming.

✻ Take a good, hard look at your own savings. Decide how much you can step up the amount of money you're setting aside every month. It's wise to allocate 15 to 20 percent of each of your paychecks to a wedding fund from the day you get engaged.

✻ Look into transferring some savings into a high-yield account or a six- or twelve-month CD. (Just make sure it matures in time to pay your vendors!)

✻ However, *do not* sink all your savings into this wedding. And don't even think about going into debt. It really sucks to start your life together under the dark cloud of financial strain. If you're tempted to use credit, make a list of all the things you might want to do in the year *after* the wedding—take trips, buy a home, get a dog, have a baby (eek!)—and imagine how it might feel to be unable to afford them. Think about how much better it would feel to go into married life feeling flush.

* The more "real" quotes you get from vendors before creating your budget, the more accurate and useful that budget will be. When you have to estimate an expense, be generous, adding 10 to 15 percent on top of your initial guess.

* Set aside 10 percent of your total budget for miscellaneous costs. Unexpected expenses will crop up, no matter how comprehensive your thinking is at the outset.

* When you log expenditures, round up to the nearest five or ten dollars.

* Adopt small savers' tricks: Consider rounding up the amount you record in your check register to the nearest dollar every time you write a check or record a debit (for expenses wedding-related or otherwise), so a little padding begins to accumulate in your checking account. Start putting all your spare change into a jar to be converted into fun money for your honeymoon.

* One quick way to decide if something is worth its lump-sum price is to determine the unit cost—just break every expense down into its smallest increment. For example, if a florist is asking for $3,000 to do the wedding party's flowers, divide that by the number of bouquets and see if it's a shocking figure. If a band wants $5,000 to play, divide that by the number of hours they'll be playing. You can even divide the hourly rate by the number of guests, to see what your hourly cost of entertaining each guest will be.

Less Is More

As you plan, the one thing you will fight over and over again is escalation: rising costs, a ballooning guest list, more and more bells and whistles and "extras." I've yet to meet a bride and groom who say their wedding turned out smaller than they imagined.

And although the best weddings do have a cohesive look and feel, that doesn't necessarily mean "theme"—this isn't a seven-year-old's birthday, or a sorority date party. It's easy to lose sight of the simple, elegant little wedding in the midst of our current consumer frenzy, but remember that it's fine if your "theme" is just "We're getting married!" The venue you choose, the time of year, and you and your fiancé's unique backgrounds, interests, and personalities make for plenty of mood-setting material. If you do articulate a theme, don't worry it to death. Two or three notes are fine.

In general, *use less.* Do you really need confetti, birdseed, *and* butterflies? Do guests really need favors? As you're faced with each new decision, decide whether you really need something or just *think* you need something because you saw it in a magazine, or at someone else's wedding. It's the party-planning equivalent of the time-honored fashion maxim: put on all your accessories and jewelry, then look in the mirror and take one thing off.

"WE DID" Advice From Real Couples

"Part of what we're into is not just environmentalism, but sustainability and social responsibility. We're pretty proud of the fact that our invitations were designed and printed by people we know, on 100-percent-recycled paper with soy-based ink, and we used reply postcards rather than cards with envelopes. My suit was made out of hemp, and on our Web site we asked guests not to buy anything new to wear to the wedding. Lots of people came up to Tybe to tell her that they'd honored our request. It's hard to do something completely environmentally friendly in a place where most people are going to have to use cars, but we booked rooms at hotels nearby [the wedding venue] so most people stayed within a few minutes' drive."

—Judd Franklin, New York, on his Los Angeles wedding to wife Tybe

Green Is the New White

Let's consider the planet for a minute. Go back to that "average" wedding cost. How much damage do you think you could do with $26,000? According to Climate Care, a British organization that sells carbon offsets, the average wedding emits around 14.5 tons of CO_2—markedly more than the 12 tons emitted by the average person during a whole year. And then there's the cost in trees, water, and fuel; pollution from things like printing and pesticides used on flowers; and the amount of waste sent to the landfill. DIY weddings, however, are generally easier on the environment. In each chapter, I'll discuss specific ways to tread lightly, but here are some big-picture ideas:

- Choose a nonprofit venue, such as a park or museum. We had our wedding at a lodge run by the National Arbor Day Foundation, a nonprofit organization dedicated to planting trees. Not only did every dollar of profit go toward greening the earth, but the facility itself was also very environmentally friendly: heating and cooling derived from wood chips burned on site; efficient plumbing and light fixtures; recycling bins in the rooms.

- Choosing any venue with inherently beautiful spaces—indoors or out—automatically saves money, resources, and CO_2 emissions because the site needs little or no decoration.

- Have your ceremony and reception in the same place so guests don't have to drive or be transported from one place to another. Even better, find a venue with ceremony space, reception space, and guest rooms all at the same facility, or within walking distance of one another. (Bonus points if the venue has airport shuttles so out-of-town guests needn't bother renting cars.)

- Think about the fuel costs and CO_2 emissions that accompany destination weddings. Can you pick a place where a lot of your guests already live? If you choose a destination wedding, how eco-friendly is your venue? Strive for sustainable tourism.

- Borrow or rent anything and everything you can, instead of buying new. For attire and jewelry, go heirloom or vintage. If you're buying a new dress or suit, organic cotton and hemp are the most responsible choices.

- Choose organic and, ideally, locally grown food and flowers.

- Choose wood-free or 100-percent-recycled paper products, and soy-based inks (like we did to print this book).

- Don't use disposable plates, glasses, cutlery, or napkins unless absolutely necessary. If you must, buy renewable and/or biodegradable products from a vendor like www.greenhome.com.

- Before you buy anything at all, from favors to bottles of water for your guests' hotel-room goody bags, ask yourself, Will this end up in a landfill?

- Consider contributing money toward carbon offsets for guests' travel in lieu of favors—check out www.gocarbonzero.org or www.terrapass.com.

- Register at small, local retailers for domestically made and environmentally friendly goods, or skip the registry altogether and tell guests "no gifts, please." If you register through the I Do Foundation (www.idofoundation.org), retailers will kick back a portion of sales to environmental (or other) charities of your choice. I went that route and was pretty happy with it, but I found myself feeling sheepish about the shipping: Before the gifts started arriving, I hadn't considered the emissions from all those planes and trucks, or the excessive, wasteful packaging. Quite a recycling challenge!

The best news is that, in many ways, what's good for the environment is also good for your wallet—especially when it involves making do with less. For more ideas and information, go to www.organic weddings.com or www.portovert.com.

Set Your Priorities

Deciding what's most important to you is what makes your vision of your event begin to come to life. Your budget begins to crystallize, and the planning process cranks into gear. If you're gaga for flowers, you clearly deserve a wedding filled with lush blooms. If you're a stationery freak, then invites will be your "thing." (Every bride has one . . . or two.) And so on and so forth—you know what you love. It's usually harder to determine what's less important, especially when you're bombarded with messages from advertisers and vendors that make every little item seem vital. So I suggest breaking things out into three categories: high, medium, and low priority.

Here's an example:

HIGH PRIORITY	MEDIUM PRIORITY	LOW PRIORITY
Beautiful setting/venue	Attire	Favors
Photos/video	Invitations	Cake
Food/liquor	Flowers	

Note that this list speaks only to your heart's desire—not to how you might allocate your precious time and money. Your next step is to indicate which items on this list should get more of your money—the things that you or someone you know couldn't satisfactorily provide under any circumstances—and which should get more of your time.

But here's the thing: You can't possibly make such detailed notes until you've begun to tally up your existing resources (again, the interdependence). So, before you get too far into the planning process, you'll want to round up the troops.

Set Your Team

Remember, you're not in this alone. DIY doesn't mean you have to do it *all* yourself. It's time to make a list of all the skills you have on tap, and put together your wedding "team." If you expand your field of vision, you may find that you've got more to work with than you think. You know what your skills and interests are, and those of your spouse-to-be and your immediate families. Beyond that, think about all your friends, and all your networks, and your families' networks.

Is there a . . .

FLORIST	JEWELRY DESIGNER
GRAPHIC DESIGNER	WOODWORKER
ARTIST	MUSICIAN
SEAMSTRESS	DJ
BAKER	PHOTOGRAPHER
CALLIGRAPHER	CLERGYPERSON

. . . in the house?

Remember that a talented amateur can often work just as well as a professional. Don't rule out anyone who could provide you with a high-quality service at a significantly reduced rate.

Now, keep thinking. Who are your downright crafty friends, the ones who are always good for ideas and/or manpower? The great cook, the friend with a knack for decorating, the pal with perfect penmanship? Do you know a hotel, motel, or bed-and-breakfast owner, or anyone who owns a fabulous piece of property that would make a good venue for the wedding? Make a list of anyone on whom you may be able to lean. Now match up your prioritized tasks with the resources you've assembled.

As far as jobs for you and your spouse-to-be, now's the time to pick whatever you naturally gravitate toward—whatever will give you the most pleasure and help you feel most connected to the wedding.

Your annotated priority list might look like this:

High Priority

RECEPTION VENUE: Definitely want great urban setting with view. Check availability and cost of renting apartment roof deck and setting up tent for partial cover. If it's out of the question, launch full search for locations with views. Willing to spend $ here.

PHOTOS/VIDEO: Best childhood friend Bill is a photojournalist. Pay for film and processing; hire separate videographer (need one who's reasonably priced; ask Bill for referral).

FOOD/LIQUOR: Don't want to bother. Hire great caterer. Can we buy our own liquor to cut costs? Make sure to tell caterer that our venue has no kitchen on site.

Medium Priority

ATTIRE: Attempt to find reasonably priced vintage cocktail dress. Excuse to shop! Buy new black suit for hubby-to-be. Make jewelry for bridesmaids and cuff links for groomsmen; these can double as gifts.

INVITATIONS: Design and order ourselves, online. Hubby-to-be has great eye for design.

FLOWERS: Sister offered to handle them—she can go for it. Work with her to establish reasonable budget.

Low Priority

FAVORS: Skip entirely

CAKE: Shoot for potluck sweets table (our moms' friends will go crazy), accented by one or two items from caterer if necessary. Make sure caterers are OK with outside desserts.

At this point, you should have a decent idea of the helpers you'll need to hire from outside your circle. Note: That doesn't necessarily mean "professionals." Throughout the book, I'll give detailed suggestions for finding alternatives to traditional wedding vendors.

There Is No "Irate" in Team

It's vital to recruit helpers for your DIY wedding but with something this important, tensions can run high. So how do you make sure that your friends will still be speaking to you post-honeymoon?

First, don't make assignments based on talent alone. Consider psychology and personality as well. For example, a friend who has trouble meeting deadlines probably should not be assigned to make the bridesmaids' dresses. Make sure that the job you're doling out is something the friend can handle.

Keeping your expectations reasonable will go a long way toward maintaining your sanity. Try to stay as plugged in to reality as possible, and to stay in touch with the actual skill levels of the people who are working for you. (Going easy on the wedding magazines will help.) If you have a pet peeve or there's something you definitely do not want—say, purple flowers in the bouquets—speak up at the outset, and reiterate it as you go along (nicely and respectfully, of course). And if the job you're assigning is something big, create a schedule that includes check-ins along the way, so you can monitor progress. Nobody likes to be micromanaged, but everyone can use clear direction and support. (And no one can read your mind.) Tell your helpers you need them to complete their (nonperishable) tasks at least two weeks before you really need them done.

Finally, make sure your team feels involved and appreciated every step of the way. When someone agrees to provide a service, send a handwritten note that says something like "Thank you so much for agreeing to photograph our wedding! We're really excited to be working with you, and so thrilled that you will be an integral part of our important day." On the wedding day, give your helper a small gift, as you would any other member of the wedding party, along with another handwritten note.

And if, goodness forbid, something turns out not at all the way you imagined, and it's too late to make a change, grit your teeth, and be gracious. No snits.

Delegate, from Day One to Wedding Day

Being a bride or groom is difficult enough if all you have to do is show up. Imagine how it will be if you're also responsible for a huge to-do list that seems to get longer every day. If you're the DIY type, be forewarned that, no matter how enthusiastic you are right now, you may want less and less to do with the planning and coordinating as the day draws near. So it's crucial that you build in a support system that includes not only the people who have specific jobs but also a gang of willing and able generalists.

One of the loveliest things about the DIY wedding is that there's nobody but your nearest and dearest in your inner circle on the big day. But that doesn't mean you don't need the help that a wedding coordinator would provide. For this reason, it's crucial that you ask your bridesmaids (if you have them) for support, and, more important, name a deputy—not your spouse, and nobody's parent—who can make decisions and execute tasks for you, if need be, on the day before, the day of, and the day after the wedding. Choose someone with whom you communicate and work well, someone who will be able to tell when you need him or her to step in. Someone who will know when to bring something to your attention, and when to let you be. Someone whose taste and judgment you trust. This is a good job for a maid of honor, best man, sibling, or anyone else who is very close to you and would be happy to do the honors.

But let me be clear: the fact that you have given someone a title doesn't mean he or she automatically knows what you expect. Have a specific conversation in which you ask "Will you be my right hand?" Describe in detail the things you want this person to handle.

Next, make a list of time- and labor-intensive tasks, from assembling invitations and favors in the months or weeks leading up to the wedding to decorating the reception space on the wedding day. Review the list of possible helpers that you created earlier, and add anyone else who's expressed willingness to help out along the way. Remember that people being called up for duty should have ample notice.

To make things run smoothly on the wedding day, and to ensure that you're using all your volunteer resources, I suggest crafting a comprehensive document (and making copies for anyone whose name appears on it) that starts with the rehearsal, ends with any morning-after activities, and includes the following:

* A schedule of what's happening when. (Level of detail is up to you, but it will likely vary from, say, hour-long increments the morning of the wedding to fifteen- or thirty-minute increments during the wedding itself and the reception.)

* Notes on who's taking care of each task.

* Cell phone numbers for everybody.

You'll also encounter lots of on-the-spot volunteers—people who ask (with various degrees of sincerity), "How can I help?" Keep a running list of short-term tasks—such as pricing tent vendors, or looking for a particular color of ribbon—that you can hand out as necessary to the people who really mean it. Inevitably, no matter how organized you are, when you get down to the wedding weekend, you will still have lots of chores to do, and new ones popping up with every passing minute. Here's a tip from one super-organized bride: Keep a stack of index cards and a marker on hand, and, as tasks crop up, write one on each card. Then, when volunteers ask what they can do, hand them a card and send them on their way! (Don't forget to jot down what job you assigned to whom.) See "DIY Team Assignments" (page 216) for a full list of jobs you may want to assign.

A WORD ABOUT CREATIVE SCUFFLES

When you're getting wedding help from someone close to you on, say, designing an invitation or coming up with a floral scheme, communication can get tricky. Unlike in a traditional vendor/client relationship, you may not feel comfortable telling your pal to go back to the drawing board, especially if the work is very time consuming, and even more so if they're doing it for you for free. But you may also be extra miserable if something is clashing with your vision of the big day. So, if you have strong opinions, it's best to state them up front. If it's your spouse-to-be you're working with, communicate as clearly as you know how, and try to find a way to merge your two visions into something that works for both of you. If you find yourselves butting heads, there are two basic solutions: Compromise, or follow the "whoever cares more wins" school of thought..

"WE DID" Advice From Real Couples

"He came home from work with a[n invitation] design. It was actually very cool, but modern—I was in a more traditional phase, and the feel didn't match anything else in the wedding. Blame it on the stress of law school, or just my usual psychotic tendencies, but when he pulled it out to show me, I didn't say a word. I just started crying. He just stared at me, probably wondering if he was making the right call in the whole marriage thing. The next day at work, he started working on the new design. He said his boss walked by and said, 'I could have told you to go with the flowers the first time.' Jason says I'm the only client he's ever made cry. The second version, however, was beautiful."

—Jill Robertson, San Francisco, on working with her graphic-designer husband, Jason

BEG, BARTER, OR STEAL

It's best not to ask for any favors that you can't repay one way or another. Inner-circle contacts may do work for your wedding as a gift or at a substantial discount—though you never should assume they're doing so. If you're considering asking for a favor, take a second to make sure that it's not out of line—if this person were asking the same of you, how would you feel? Whatever you do, don't take advantage of anyone. One way to keep things even is to consider bartering: What good or service could you, or someone in your family, provide the other person in return? Among your friends—since groups of people tend to get married in packs—what can you do for one another? People are surprisingly open to bartering, if you ask.

Get Inspired

With your priorities straight, your resources identified, and your troops lined up, you can move on to the more creative stuff. A great way to begin to conjure the look and feel of your wedding is to create an inspiration board, or "mood" board. Designers (interior, fashion, graphic, all of 'em) use bulletin or magnetized boards full of images and words to bring concepts to life. For wedding planning, it's a great place to compile all the colors, textures, and images that inspire you: magazine pages, invitations and stationery, paper samples, greeting cards, paint chips, photos, swatches of fabric. Display anything you love to look at that will help create an image in your mind. Because it hangs on your wall like a billboard, you can glance at it as you go about your day. Ordinary moments at home morph into thinking and dreaming opportunities, and these may help you determine which of your ideas have "legs," and what you might get bored with quickly. It's an ever-evolving collage—just add what feels right, and take away what doesn't. When it all seems to hang together, you're ready to start planning.

"Fine and dandy," you say . . . "but I have a job, and a life, and now a million appointments and obligations related to this wedding, which is definitely not going to get planned by my staring at a wall." Indeed. Which is why you might prefer a way to gather inspiration and information on the go. It's too tedious to three-hole-punch everything (and too cumbersome to haul around a heavy binder), and it's too easy for things to slip out of a file folder. So I suggest organizing your to-do lists, notes, bits of inspiration, and other wedding ephemera in a large (at least legal-sized), sturdy zippered envelope or pouch made out of vinyl or mesh. You can find them at the Container Store or office-supply stores. (The brand I used was Design Ideas.) Fill it up with everything from poems to postcards to matchbook covers, and purge often—once you've made a decision in a particular area, get rid of all the other options you've been hoarding.

Magazine-Rack Racket

Wedding magazines are (hopefully) a one-time phenomenon in your life; as such, you are entitled to as many as you can get your paws on. They certainly can be full of inspiration and ideas—some more so than others. But at a certain point, well, they can threaten to take over your home. To avoid clutter, and the classic "Where the &*$# did I see that?!" frustration, try "tear-sheeting" a magazine page the second you see something you love. Stick the torn-out pages on your inspiration board or tuck them into your pouch. Then recycle the rest of the magazine, or pass it on to a friend.

But do consider that a steady diet of wedding mags can give even the most centered bride nervous indigestion. They're the wedding industry's most powerful tool for convincing you that you need things you really don't. Remember that guests care more about seeing you and the groom happy than they do about tiny details.

For safety's sake, I limited my consumption to the wedding bible: *Martha Stewart Weddings*. Of course, I flipped through plenty of other glossies at the newsstand, but I didn't buy. You may notice, as I did, that after a while all wedding magazines start to look the same. In fact, I got just as much wedding inspiration from fashion, home decor, and travel magazines, which are equally good—or better—at bringing a mood to life, and they're generally more exciting and evocative to boot.

Look and Feel

Your wedding's personality is going to emerge and evolve with each decision you make. But right now, before you get anywhere near the sign-on-the-dotted-line stage, is the time to step back and imagine all the different scenarios that could make you happy. I'm sure you're doing that automatically—your mind probably started drifting toward possible venues the minute that ring landed on your finger. But take your time, and think it through. Should it be indoors or out? Casual or fancy? Will you greet your guests on the beach, on a mountaintop, or in a vineyard? Will the event be inspired by a beloved place, or an annual event? A hometown, or an adopted city? A shared hobby or profession? A cultural heritage, or just a culture you admire?

Our wedding was very simple and didn't have anything I'd call a "theme," so we relied heavily on the simple beauty of the outdoors, and the power of color, manifested in our wedding party's attire and our flowers. When you're prowling around for inspiration, color is an excellent avenue to wander down. What colors make you ecstatically happy? What colors remind you of places you love? A caveat, though: while some brides get as attached to their "colors" as a high-school cheerleader might, adopting a more flexible attitude is going to net you a better-looking wedding, with more visual depth. It's best to avoid a style that's too "matchy," with every last detail coordinated, and also a look that's too "mixy," with too many dissonant colors. Pick whatever you like, but make sure it works with, not against, the setting and that it makes sense for the season. The best place to see all the colors in the rainbow—and make off with samples—is the paint display at a hardware store. You can comb the samples to your heart's content and take them home to live with them for a while. (Fabric stores are good for inspiration too.) If you need to communicate color information to faraway friends or wedding-party members, mail them the appropriate paint chips. Don't rely on how things look online—the colors you see on a computer screen aren't true to life.

Get Moving

Now that you've built an image of the big day in your head, it's time to make the big decisions: roughly how many people will attend, where it will take place, and when it will happen. All your other planning decisions will flow from these three choices, which are, yep, *interdependent*.

The People

It's smart to rough out an ideal guest list as early as possible—and prepare to haggle over it until the day the invitations go in the mail. Kidding! (Sort of.) Make a list of people you *must* invite and another list of people you'd *like* to invite. Gather preliminary lists of names from your families as soon as possible. Consider costs and the impact on the wedding's vibe as your numbers grow. Obviously, the smaller the wedding, the easier it is to DIY. Two hundred guests is probably the upper limit for an event you're going to pull off with a minimum of professional help.

It's always tricky to estimate how many of the invited guests will show up. I've seen estimates ranging from 50 to 90 percent, depending on too many factors to name. But the best general rule I've encountered is that you'll have roughly as many guests as the number of envelopes you address. Old wedding coordinators' tale? Complicated statistical analysis? Beats me, but it works. With our wedding, it was too low by 20 people—what I'd call the outside edge of an acceptable margin of error. But it gave us a decent number to work with until we started getting real data.

The Place

Picking the right setting is the best thing you can do for your wedding. A place that is gorgeous when empty is only going to get more so when it's filled with an ecstatic bride and groom and their merry guests. Plus, the better it looks on its own, the less you need to adorn it, which means less work and less expense. Consider a foolproof natural setting—a forest, mountaintop, lakeside dock, or beach. Or, if you don't want to stress about the weather, a restaurant, club, or loft with big windows and great views of water, sunset, or city skyline. If you're getting married around the holidays, consider someplace that will already be tastefully decorated with greenery and lights. The possibilities are endless. Just keep your eyes open when you go to look at possible venues and see how "turnkey" they are: could you just walk in and have the wedding there tomorrow?

Do consider that where you choose to have the wedding may influence how much you can DIY. Many venues require you to use their own catering and/or bar services. And, since you and your team may be doing a lot of the setup, you'll want to inquire about access to the venue before your event. You don't want to be arranging centerpieces twenty minutes before the ceremony.

Also, try to at least have a ballpark number of guests in mind before you begin your venue search so you don't go falling in love with something that's too small or too big.

And one final thing to consider: good lighting is absolutely key to a great event. That doesn't mean that you need to hire a lighting designer, but when you're scoping venues, do note a few things: How much natural light does the space get? From which directions? Is the overhead lighting flattering? Flexible? Are the lights on dimmers? Can you provide your own lighting instead? If portions of the event will take place outside, when's sunrise/sunset/moonrise on the dates you're considering? What phase will the moon be in the day you're thinking of getting married? (A full moon adds a magical—and wild—touch to a wedding.) You can find all this information on the Web. If possible, visit all of your possible venues at the hours you'd be using them to get a true picture of the lighting.

The Date

Have you had a target month or day in mind from the minute you got engaged? Great—but try to be flexible. When you find a venue you like, inquire immediately about availability. If you have the luxury of choice, work with the seasons, choosing the time of year that best flatters your venue. Don't be shy about asking questions, such as "Can you show me pictures of past winter weddings?" "How late does it stay warm in the fall?" "What's going to be blooming in May, and in what colors?" "What's this bush over here, and how will it look on my wedding day?" Ideally, nature will set a beautiful stage for your wedding, with related color choices, flowers, and menu all flowing from the look of your wedding venue on the day you wed. The bonus: you'll get higher quality at a lower price when you use flowers and food in season, and it's better for the environment that way, too.

Make sure you ask all the major players about their availability before you set a date. That means both families (parents and siblings), and anyone whom you're going to ask to be in your wedding party. If you must have a certain officiant (more on that in Chapter Nine), you'll also want to check with that person. Keep holidays, big days like the Super Bowl, and peak airfare times in mind. Weddings on weeknights, Fridays, and Sundays are gaining in popularity, and they can certainly save you money, but they may ratchet up the expenses for your guests, since they may have to take time off work and incur extra hotel costs. Ask yourself, "If I were a guest at this wedding, is there anything about the scheduling or timing that would annoy me?" When you weigh all the factors, you may conclude that Saturday is still the best day for a wedding. To cut costs, consider Saturday morning or afternoon instead of the evening, or early enough on Sunday so people can travel home afterward.

Finally, before you sign on the dotted line for a particular venue, be sure to take any disabled or elderly guests into account. Think about it in both macro (is there anyone important for whom travel is difficult?) and micro (how accessible are the ceremony and reception spaces, and what kind of travel is required to get from one to the other?) terms.

Deep Breath: Pat Yourself on the Back

Whew—what a process! Did you ever imagine it would be this complicated? It's simply exhausting to hold all these interlocking variables in your mind. But look at everything you've accomplished: You've set your priorities, assembled your DIY team, secured your venue, established your wedding date, determined the broad strokes of your budget, and maybe locked in the cost of your venue, if applicable. *You may have even sent in a deposit.* (Holy crap! It's happening!) These are *huge* accomplishments. I promise that these early decisions really are the bulk of your wedding work—the intellectual and psychological work, anyway, which are the hardest kinds—and that your discipline and coordination here will pay off later. Now you can begin to fill in the rest of your budget numbers and sail on toward the fun stuff. But, before you proceed, take a moment to celebrate with your fiancé. (It'd make a nice antidote if, you know, you might happen to be having any little disagreements or slightly fraught conversations or anything like that. Just in case.) Splurge on a nice dinner. Pop open a bottle of bubbly. And breathe.

ATTIRE

CHAPTER TWO

Most couples, even if they're wildly daring in other areas, still play it safe with wedding attire: white bridal gowns, matching dresses for the 'maids, rented tuxes for the men. Classic? Sure. Compulsory? Nope. I'm here to tell you that, when it comes to your attire, it really is *your* day—more so than in any other area of wedding planning. You can, and should, wear whatever you please. Plus, there are so many creative ways to make your wedding party stand out from the rest of your guests, infuse your wedding with DIY spirit, *and* save money at the same time that it's almost criminal *not* to bust out of the wedding-attire mold, at least a little bit.

This chapter will help you figure out your unique look, and the look of the entire wedding party, with DIY flair. But by no means do you have to go whole hog—you could just make your own veil, add a handmade sash to your dress, or give your groom and his groomsmen handmade cuff links. You don't even have to make anything at all. Wearing things that have sentimental value is very DIY. And inspiration is everywhere: Maybe you'll build your concept off an heirloom cameo ring, a swatch of chintz from a chaise longue, a well-loved cashmere sweater, a vintage postcard from a seaside resort. It's the spirit of DIY, rather than the letter, that shakes things up and makes the magic happen. Begin by thinking about what might look stunning against the backdrop you've established, and let your imagination run free.

Here Comes the Dress

Of all the many wedding-day totems, the bride's dress is arguably the most sacred. Let the tent fly away, the cake collapse, and the flowers wilt—as long as all's well with the dress, your bridal glow should be bulletproof. That said, if you're thinking of going the DIY route, be honest about your limits in this arena. If you've never sewn a stitch but still want a handmade dress, find yourself a dressmaker—be she a friend or a professional for hire. If you go vintage, read on for tips on finding the highest-quality garments. And, in case you want to rework a relative's dress, I've pulled together some handy guidance.

Tip: There's no hard-and-fast rule for when to begin dress hunting, because everyone's search unfolds differently. But if you want your dress to mesh with the rest of the event, I'd make it the second big task you tackle, immediately after cementing the wedding date and place.

Wedding-Dress Alternatives

One way to DIY is to break out of the long-white-dress mold. Try . . .

* A bridesmaid's dress or two-piece outfit in a pale color (blush, icy blue, champagne) as a wedding dress (often available at a tiny fraction of the cost of wedding-dress prices, and virtually indistinguishable in quality)

* A suit made of lace, satin, or creamy wool bouclé, depending on the season and time of day

* Skipping the white altogether. Many brides aren't brave enough, but a colored wedding dress looks divine and it really opens up your options when shopping for something vintage. (If you're looking for more justification, remember that in many cultures, wedding dresses aren't white—in fact, white is a funeral color in China!) You could go bold, of course, or subtle—a slinky cocktail dress in a metallic, a neutral color, or even black can be stunning on a bride.

✳ Borrow or rent something outrageous or just plain fabulous from a theater company, costume shop, or store that rents vintage clothing.

Vintage

A vintage dress adds flavor to any wedding. You could go with a swingy sixties minidress or a slinky bias-cut thirties gown. There are so many options out there, and pawing through them is the ultimate treasure hunt. When you find your prize, you can wear it "as is" or rework it into a divine custom creation. And, no, it doesn't matter if it's truly vintage or more like preowned—if you spot something you love, who cares when it was made, or who else has worn it? No one needs to know where it came from, unless, of course, you're so proud of your bargain-hunting skills that you want to tell the world.

Before I go into details on where to find and how to spot vintage honeys, keep in mind one very important thing: A beautifully made dress can be a worthwhile investment even if it needs a few repairs or alterations. You can shorten a skirt, remove the sleeves, add a sash, fortify the top of a strapless dress with extra boning, or cut out layers of tulle to give the dress a different line. Sequins or beads can always be moved, taken off, or added. (In fact, you can save a lot of money by buying an unadorned dress and adding beading or other embellishments yourself.) If the dress has good genes to begin with, and you've got a talented tailor in your arsenal, the possibilities are endless.

Keep in mind, too, that size is less important than it might seem, *as long as the garment is too big rather than too small.* Anything that requires inordinate wriggling or squeezing in order to zip it up should go back on the rack for someone else to enjoy, unless you're confident that there's adequate seam allowance for alterations (get a professional opinion to make sure). But most dresses that are a few sizes too big can easily be cut down to fit.

Vintage Shopping List

If you're shopping for a vintage or secondhand wedding dress, don't leave home without a big ol' purse, stocked with:

- A large compact or small hand mirror, to compensate for inadequate fitting-room mirrors.

- A digital camera—though be sure to ask the sales staff for permission to photograph their merchandise.

- The best bras in your arsenal.

- A "foundation garment," if you're interested in something from the sixties or before, because many dresses from years past were designed for girdle-wearing gals. Thank goodness for spandex! Just go to a department store with a good intimates section and ask the nice lady what she has in body shapers.

- Heels, roughly the height you hope to wear with your dress, so you can see its true length.

- A candid friend, to take pictures of you and give honest (but kind) feedback.

- Notebook and pen for recording what you saw, and *where*—this is very important when you are looking at one-of-a-kind items.

- Cash. If you're serious about buying a vintage dress, you may need to make a quick decision, and you may find yourself in a cash-only situation. Even if the store accepts credit cards, the owner may prefer cash as a means of avoiding credit-card processing fees, and you may find that you can get the price down a bit if you offer to pay that way. In general, it never hurts to try to haggle, as long as you're respectful. A warm smile and a friendly "Is this the best you can do?" can help you sniff out if there's room to negotiate.

Where to Look

Vintage clothing stores aren't your only options. Thrift, charity, and consignment (different from the first two because the seller only gets money if the item sells, and therefore the merch is usually better organized and presented) shops, eBay, and marketplaces on wedding Web sites can all net you some beautiful options. (However, if you've never purchased used clothing online before, this probably isn't a good time for your maiden voyage, unless it's a low-cost item and you're prepared to eat the purchase price in the event that it's a bust.) See "Resources" on page 218 for places to start the hunt.

Tip: Savvy DIYers shop the thrift stores outside of major urban areas, where prices are lower and the merchandise isn't as picked over. ∽

How to spot a worthwhile investment:

❶ Start with the fabric. Hunt for a fabric content label, and, if you find one, read it carefully. Natural fabrics (silk, cotton, wool) are superior to synthetics. Then rub it between your fingers—that's the "hand feel." After petting enough fabric, you'll begin to distinguish high quality from low. Each material has its unique attributes: silk shantung should feel heavy and substantial, lace should be delicate and lightweight, and satin should be smooth and free of snags. But the bottom line is that high-quality fabric will feel good in your hand; it's really as simple as that. Of course, great fabric looks beautiful, too, and it drapes well on the body.

❷ Look for a designer's label, and make a note of what it says. You may recognize the maker's name immediately, but if you don't, do some research—you may be in for a nice surprise. The maker's name will probably influence the cost of the item, but depending on where you're shopping, you may know more about what it's really worth than the person who priced it does. (Note: Handmade garments often don't have any labels inside them at all; consult an expert if you're not sure what you're looking at.)

❸ Check the seams—are they double-stitched or single-stitched? (Double-stitched seams are indicative of fine workmanship.) Either way, how are they holding up? Could they withstand a night of dancing?

4 Inspect the garment for obvious signs of wear—pilling, thinned fabric in places, tears, and holes—and for stains. Look more closely than you think is necessary, and then look again. If it's dark in the store, ask the salesperson if you may take it up by the front window, or even outdoors. Ideally, get a look at the dress in the kind of light you'll have on your wedding day.

5 If the dress has beading or other detail work, check the quality. Pull (gently!) on beads to see how firmly they are attached. Look to see how many are missing. (If the garment is old, it's almost guaranteed that some will have fallen off. But don't fret—if you can find similar or complementary beads, you or a seamstress can easily replace them.)

When you find something that you think might work, try it on in front of a well-lit three-way mirror. If one isn't available, use a friend and a hand mirror to get a look at your backside. Make notes about what you like about the dress, and what you wish you could change. Keep in mind that if the dress will need any alterations, from a little tuck to a structural overhaul, it's risky to make the purchase until you've lined up a talented tailor or seamstress (more on that in a minute), described your vision, and gotten his or her take on how much skill, time, and money the alterations will require.

In general, if it fits like anything other than your own skin, or needs repairs, and the cost is more than you're prepared to lose, don't buy it until you've gotten an opinion from someone you trust on how flattering it is (or could be, with alterations) and a tailor's thoughts and estimate. Ask the shopkeepers to hold it for you while you secure the necessary information.

Honoring an Heirloom

Think Mom's dress won't work? Think again. All of the previous advice can also be applied to a family heirloom—*as long as the dress's original owner is OK with the garment being altered.* If you're taking things away—sleeves, skirt, train—consider having the extra fabric made into a keepsake pillow, wall hanging, or mat for a wedding photo.

You might even try putting photos of all the brides who have worn the dress into one frame, surrounded by a mat made out of the fabric, and present your creation to the previous owner of the dress.

Tip: Bleach is much too harsh for aged or delicate white fabrics—instead, try brightening them with old-fashioned bluing. It's affordable, nontoxic, and biodegradable. Try Mrs. Stewart's Bluing (www.mrsstewart.com) or Bluette, available at grocery stores.

SPOTTING A KEEPER

Here's how to spot a diamond in the rough—and avoid a dud.

Snap it up—it's easy to fix.

· Tears on a seam · Missing beadwork or sequins
· Too long · Broken zipper · Needs brightening—
and it's a natural fiber

Walk away—it'll never look smashing.

· Tears or holes anywhere other than on a seam · Stains
· Too short · Too small (without adequate seam allowance)
· Needs brightening—and it's synthetic

"WE DID" Advice From Real Couples

"I'm building my wedding outfit around what I was wearing the day I met Thom. It was my favorite A-line skirt, turquoise with a big white floral print, with a white top, and this red necklace that's made out of giant round plastic beads. I love that outfit, and I especially love that necklace. So I'm going to wear it at the wedding! With a short white dress that has a turquoise sash. I'll carry red Gerber daisies. Done and done."

—Meredith McDonough, New York, on her wedding-day outfit

Dresses Through the Decades

Every decade has its classic fashion silhouettes, the geniuses who birthed them, and the bods that made them famous. If you hope to evoke a particular period in Western fashion history, read on to learn whom you'll be channeling.

Era: Early-to-Mid-1800s

Trend: Enter the white wedding dress, when Queen Victoria selects the shade for her own big day in 1840.

POSTER GIRL: QUEEN V HERSELF

Era: Early Twentieth Century

Trend: Edwardian T&A is the order of the day, thanks to the omnipresent corset. Lots of accessories, too.

POSTER GIRL: THE GIBSON GIRL

Era: 1920s

Trend: What corset? Flapper dresses with dropped waists and above-the-knee hemlines are all the rage.

POSTER GIRLS: ZELDA FITZGERALD AND COCO CHANEL

Era: 1930s

Trend: The privileged few who can afford new dresses opt for body-hugging, bias-cut gowns like those pioneered by Madeline Vionnet, with boat-shaped necklines for balance.

POSTER GIRLS: WALLIS SIMPSON AND MARLENE DIETRICH

Era: 1940s

Trend: Wartime rationing forces women to simplify and smile about it, lest they appear unpatriotic. Suits and stronger, mannish, military-inspired silhouettes with padded shoulders reign.

POSTER GIRL: LAUREN BACALL

Era: 1950s

Trend: The "new look," courtesy of Christian Dior, comes of age: it's a full-on return to femininity in ballerina-inspired dresses with tight waists, stiff petticoats, and flouncy skirts.

POSTER GIRLS: AUDREY HEPBURN AND JACKIE KENNEDY

Era: 1960s

Trend: Culture quake—depending on which side of the fault line you're standing on, wedding fashions are either much like those of the fifties or utterly mod, like Yoko Ono's white minidress and knee socks (at least until mid-decade, when most everybody got hip).

POSTER GIRL: YOKO ONO

Era: 1970s

Trend: Disco fever! Fashion becomes more flexible, fluid, and body-conscious; clothing incorporates ethnic influences thanks to the advent of easier air travel.

POSTER GIRLS: KATE JACKSON, FARRAH FAWCETT, JACLYN SMITH

Era: 1980s

Trend: Prep city. Frills and furbelows own the fashion world.

POSTER GIRLS: PRINCESS DI AND CAROLINE KENNEDY SCHLOSSBERG

Era: 1990s

Trend: Minimalism rules—fashion icons favor clean lines and very few decorative touches.

POSTER GIRL: CAROLYN BESSETTE KENNEDY

Era: Contemporary

Trend: Ornamentation of all types is back. In recent years, a mix of classic styling and bare skin has reigned supreme, with strapless gowns everywhere you look. Thankfully, the field is beginning to open up a bit; lace is becoming extremely popular.

POSTER GIRLS: THE CELEBRITY-BRIDE BRIGADE IN INSTYLE WEDDINGS

Tip: Go to *www.fashion-era.com for tons of period-specific inspiration.*

Tailor Made

A dress handcrafted by a sartorial savant is the ultimate in DIY luxury, even more so if it's a custom design. It's haute couture on a down-home scale. I took this approach, but on a whim. Shortly after I got engaged, I took a trip to Paris with some girlfriends. One wildly optimistic day in the Eighth Arrondissement, emboldened by too much St. Marcellin cheese and *vin rouge,* I impulsively bought a large quantity of lace. Back home, I found a designer—*two blocks from our apartment*—who turned it into a custom confection. I'd say I was unbelievably lucky that it worked out, but I think the success of the dress had as much to do with my openness of vision and flexibility about the outcome as anything else. Before you decide to go this route, think about what you want, how picky you are, and how much time you have, as well as who might do the labor (and at what skill level). As usual, the trick is to match your vision with the person who can help make it come alive.

There are two different approaches to having a dress made:

Option One:

The Semi-Pro: Say your dressmaker, whoever he or she may be, is very handy with a sewing machine, as long as the pattern already exists. In this case, carefully choose a well-crafted pattern, as well as fabric that will work with the style you've selected—or vice versa, if you've fallen in love with a fabric and want to hunt for a pattern that will show it off. Be sure to consult with your dressmaker every step of the way. (Or, ideally, go shopping together.)

Option Two:

The Pro: If your dressmaker knows how to take a garment from concept to execution, including pattern making and draping—the whole nine yards (forgive the pun)—share your vision with him or her as soon as possible. Use tear sheets from magazines or photos of other brides to illustrate your ideas. Then, when the designer shows you sketches, sign off on the one(s) you like (or ask for any changes you'd like to see), and hunt together for the right fabric. (Or, again, work the other way around, presenting the designer with fabric at the outset and collaborating to decide how best to use it.)

TIMELESS CLASSICS

Wedding outfits in other, less-fickle cultures transcend trends and stay relevant for generations: saris from India, kimonos from Japan, barongs from the Philippines, kilts from the British Isles, soft lace dresses from Mexico. Don't be afraid to mix another culture's traditions with contemporary American favorites, whether you can lay claim to a particular heritage, are getting married on foreign soil, or just admire a far-flung land.

Tip: One good resource for all things international is Timeless Traditions: A Couple's Guide to Wedding Customs Around the World, *by Lisl M. Spangenberg.*

Finding a Seamstress or Designer

If you don't know someone who can help you bring your dress to life, don't despair. There are several good places to look. Start with boutiques that specialize in wedding dresses—places that sell dresses off the rack may employ a house designer as well, or a salesperson who makes dresses on the side.

Don't be afraid to try your local fabric stores (from high-end to low). The sales staff will surely know of talented seamstresses who work out of their homes, or they will know how to put you in touch with someone who can make a referral.

Finally, scope out local fashion schools or design colleges. Find the employment offices at these schools and tack notes on their bulletin boards (real or Internet), or go to the administration office and ask to speak to a professor who teaches a dressmaking class. He or she should be able to point you toward a talented student, or perhaps you'll end up hiring the professor!

Beware of less-targeted methods of finding someone to make you a dress, such as posting on Craigslist. If you take that approach, you may wind up with too many options to slog through. If you do find someone that way, however, ask for as many references as possible, and check each one.

In the end, word of mouth is always the best way to find someone good. And, if you're committed to an unorthodox approach, remember to be flexible, resourceful, and patient.

Couture and Compatibility

If you and the person making your dress are simpatico, it can be a wonderful experience. If you're sparring, it can be torture. Here are a few pointers on choosing well, and keeping the relationship copacetic.

First, realistically assess your budget and your tolerance for risk. Ask around for recommendations, and then go with the most experienced person you can afford. Skimp only if your wallet demands it and your stomach lining can take it. Second, I highly recommend meeting the candidate in person before you decide to work together. When you meet, you'll probably get a sense of the dressmaker's personal style from what he or she is wearing, and this may give you a clue to whether it's a fit. However, the person may have more range than is immediately apparent. Be open-minded, but exercise due diligence. When you meet, describe what you're looking for in as much detail as possible. Ask to see the dressmaker's portfolio, or, better yet, a few garments he or she has created. Finally, ask if he or she is willing to refer you to past clients, and then call them up and get the scoop.

When you think you've found a match, agree on a schedule that feels comfortable. You'll want to plan for at least three to five fittings along the way, depending on the complexity of the dress, plus pattern consultations and fabric-finding missions, if necessary. (One way to tell if dressmakers are picky and dedicated to their craft is that they'll want more fittings than you do. The woman who made my dress was a perfectionist—lucky me.) Remember to take your datebook to the initial meeting, and to every one after that. As you move through the process, don't leave even one fitting without getting the next on your calendar. And pad your deadline! Aim to schedule the final fitting for about two weeks before the wedding. It can be problematic to schedule it much earlier than that, because most brides lose at least a little weight in the weeks before the wedding, but do try to give yourself a little leeway. If your dressmaker misses a deadline, be understanding—to a point. One slipped fitting date is forgivable. Two merits a firm intervention.

Finally, always put the agreement in writing. Even if the person you're working with is a friend or acquaintance, it's wise to sign at least an informal contract. (See "Contracts 101" on page 214 for more info.) And, again, even if it's a friend, attach a monetary figure to the contract, with half paid up front, and half to be paid on delivery of the finished dress. Insist on this, even if all your friend will accept is a token amount. Money keeps people honest, gives them that extra incentive to respond to deadline pressure, and can forestall feelings of resentment if a project turns out to be more complicated than one or both of you anticipated. (And it always does.)

"WE DID" Advice From Real Couples

"I couldn't stomach the idea of spending a few thousand dollars on a dress I'd only wear for one day, so I looked for alternate options. After a false start with a student at the Academy of Art in San Francisco, I learned of a woman who enjoys sewing on the side (she works in a fabric store) and we talked about a dress. Ultimately, we both agreed that a wedding dress was a little more than she was able to commit to at the time. I then freaked out and started looking online. One company said they could do it for $750 but then said that the design I wanted was actually too difficult. I contracted with another company for $350, got the dress, and hated it. It was too big, and barely recognizable. I was about to give up on having a dress made when my mom convinced me to go to an alterations store at a mall in the suburbs. As soon as I put the dress on, the seamstress started ripping. By default, she was hired. Since then I have gone to two fittings and am quite happy. The dress will resemble what I had in mind, will be fitted perfectly to me, and will come out at under $800 in total. I am adding an antique brooch, which I bought on eBay, along with a veil and tiara. If I were to do it again, I'd go to the seamstress in the mall in the first place. I never thought I'd buy my wedding dress at the mall, but there you go!"

—Sarnata Reynolds, San Francisco, on her dress quest

Questions to Ask a Dressmaker

Determine his or her rate and availability, and consider the following:

- "How many dresses have you made, or helped make?"
- "How many of those were wedding dresses?"
- "What's your basic philosophy on wedding dresses?"
- "What are your favorite styles to make?"
- "Do you tend to go for more embellishment, or less?"
- "Which is more important to you, design or comfort?"
- "Where will you make the dress?"
- "Do you have access to all the equipment you need?"
- "Are you comfortable taking on this project?"
- "May I have your references, preferably former brides you've worked with?"

Once you've got a list of references, call the people on the list and politely ask the following questions:

- "Was the project finished on time?"
- "Were you happy with the result?"
- "Is there anything I should be aware of?"
- "Do you have pictures I can see?"

Where to Find Great Patterns

Many dress designers, including Nicole Miller, Jessica McClintock, and Donna Ricco, offer wedding-dress patterns. Bridesmaid-dress patterns can work well too—just do them up in a bridal fabric. If you're looking for vintage patterns, eBay is a great source.

Where to Find Great Fabric

Most big cities have garment districts that offer treasure troves of fabric options. Remember to always ask about the fabric content, and lean on salespeople for advice about what fabrics might suit the design you have in mind. If you want to be eco-friendly, hemp and organic unbleached cotton are your best bets. Check out www.greensage.com for some options.

Where to Find Great Notions

If you're adding to an existing dress, there are a zillion ways you can go. Every fabric store has notions, or trim, but the higher-end stores will have nicer options. You can often find lots of "dead stock" notions at garage or closeout sales—you never know what you'll turn up. Consider cutting beads or other trim off of another garment and applying them to your wedding dress—that's also a sweet way to use a snippet of something from an heirloom gown.

Complete the Package

Even if you're not going DIY for the dress itself, there are plenty of other things to play with. Your veil, shoes, jewelry and other accessories, makeup, and hair are all perfect opportunities to add a personalized touch. Try wearing gloves with hand-embroidered edges; a handmade necklace, bracelet, or earrings; or an heirloom veil. Tap a talented friend to do your makeup, and another to be completely honest about whether you're wearing too much blush. Let your finishing touches be constrained only by your imagination.

Veils

Before you tackle making your own veil, research various styles online (www.veilshop.com has a good selection) and try on as many as you can (ideally, with your dress!) to see what you like.

If you want precise guidance, invest in a pattern. Vogue, Burda, Butterick, McCall's, and Simplicity all offer good veil patterns. And remember, you can make almost anything—an old brooch, some vintage buttons, a giant artificial tiger lily—into a hair accessory by hot-gluing it onto a 4-inch-wide clear plastic comb, or lashing it on with clear fishing line.

UNVEIL A TRADITION

Here's another idea: Make your veil your "something borrowed." Use a family veil (a great way to honor a relative whose dress wasn't quite your style) or start a tradition among your group of friends by passing a beautiful veil on to the woman who's getting married next.

If you chose to make your own veil, the amount of tulle you need varies according to what length you desire, and how tall you are:

* *Shoulder ("blusher"), 18 to 24 inches*

* *Waist, 30 inches*

* *Fingertip, 38 to 40 inches*

* *Floor length ("chapel"), 60 to 72 inches*

* *Cathedral, 108 inches or longer*

Turn the page for easy project instructions.

HOW TO MAKE A VEIL

Making a unique, beautiful veil is easier than you might expect. Below is a basic model that you can modify as you wish.

MATERIALS:

• Tulle, a.k.a. "bridal illusion," in 108-inch width (Tulle requires no finishing. You can make veils out of other fabrics, but you'll have to finish the raw edges.) • Weighted objects (such as books) • Dressmaker's chalk or a soft lead pencil • Sharp dressmaking shears, or a rotary cutter and cutting mat • Needle • Sturdy thread in a color that matches the tulle • Attachment mechanism: comb, headband, "bridal loops" (sold by the yard at fabric stores) • Hot glue gun, glue sticks, and fabric glue • Pearls, sequins, crystals, or other decoration (If you're getting your dress altered, save the leftovers and affix them to the veil.)

1. Lay out the tulle on a *clean*, flat surface. Fold it in half lengthwise. Place small weights along the edges to hold it in place.

2. Use the chalk or pencil to trace a curve along the bottom, slightly rounding the veil's bottom edge. Take the dressmaker's shears and cut the veil along the line you've traced, cutting inside the line if you've used pencil. Unfold the tulle.

3. Take needle and thread and sew the top (straight) edge of the tulle with a running stitch, all the way across. When you've reached the other end, cinch the two outer edges together by pulling the thread out and pushing the fabric in. (You're gathering the tulle as you would a curtain on a rod.) Once you have it all cinched up, tie off the thread securely. This process makes the top edge of the veil small so it can be attached to your comb or headband.

4. Hot glue or sew the veil to the attachment mechanism according to instructions on the package, and decorate away.

Think Outside the (Wedding-Shoe) Box

Wedding shoes can be downright heinous—clunky, poorly made—and the pretty ones are insanely overpriced. And because most people don't wear white shoes in everyday life, there aren't a lot of options outside of the wedding-shoe ghetto. Or are there?

First, do you really have to wear white shoes? Consider whether another option might work: a metallic, a pastel, a pale neutral, or even a pop of bright color, if your dress can handle it. Take shoe cues from your setting. Many an outdoorsy bride has donned cowboy boots under her dress, to delightful effect. Or what about a black patent-leather pump with an ivory satin dress for a chic nighttime wedding, a sweet patterned flat under a long dress for a small-town morning or afternoon wedding, or barely-there neutral leather sandals for poolside or beach nuptials?

However, don't think you can get away with tennis shoes or embellished "bridal" flip-flops just because you'll be wearing a floor-length dress. People will be able to see your feet, even if only in fleeting glimpses. If comfort is a concern, consider ballroom-dancing shoes—there are some pretty, strappy satin versions out there.

The trickiest thing about wedding-shoe shopping is that you usually need to see the dress and shoes together before you can make a decision, and you can't really haul around a wedding dress while you shop for shoes. And, to make things even more difficult, if your dress is being made or altered, you usually need the shoes *before* the dress itself is finished.

To really cover the waterfront on your wedding-shoe search, go online. The best sites list heel heights in the description of each shoe. (At your first fitting, make sure you think through what heel height you'll need, for dress purposes, and/or not-towering-over-groom purposes.) I found great wedding shoes at www.myglassslipper.com; see "Resources" on page 219 for more online shopping options.

HOW TO EMBELLISH A SHOE

A genius way to both add a DIY touch to a drab shoe and help tie shoes and dress together is to take any old button, cover it in the same fabric that was used to make your dress, and attach it to your shoe. This is easiest to do if you're having the dress made or have a snippet of fabric left over from alterations.

MATERIALS:

- 2 or more large, sturdy buttons (in any color, unless your fabric is sheer)
- Scraps of fabric (from your dress, or in a coordinating fabric)
- Dressmaker's shears • Hot-glue gun and glue sticks

1. Place the button facedown on the scrap of fabric and use shears to cut around it, leaving a wide enough edge to fold in tight and cover the entire back of the button, but not so much that you'll create too much extra bulk.

2. Fold one portion of the fabric over the back of the button and affix it to the button with hot glue. Continue around the rest of the button, working slowly, tucking it all together neatly. If the button has holes in it, take care that the glue doesn't seep through onto the front of the fabric.

3. Once the entire button is covered, affix it to your shoe with hot glue. You can place it almost anywhere it looks good; try the top of the foot, in the center (best for a really big button, and a dramatic look), or off to the side, near the top of your pinky toe (good for a slightly smaller button, and a more demure look). With high heels that have a closed back, gluing a button (or a row of them) on the back of the heel can make the shoe look really elegant.

4. Repeat steps 1 through 3 with the other button(s).

HOW TO GIVE HEIRLOOM JEWELRY NEW LIFE

A gorgeous way to incorporate "something old" into your wedding-day wardrobe is to wear a piece of heirloom or vintage jewelry. Start kissing up to female relatives now! But seriously: Don't despair if you don't happen to have a pristine string of pearls or art-deco drop diamond earrings in the family vault. You've surely got something pretty and interesting in your arsenal, and it's gratifying to take an old or infirm piece of jewelry and make it into something entirely new.

Here are a few snippets of inspiration:

* Those odd beads rolling around in the bottom of your jewelry box can be made into earrings. (See basic earring-making instructions on page 71.)

* A necklace can be wrapped around your wrist several times and accented with a charm.

* You can make *anything* with a hole in it into a pendant.

* You can make any brooch or pin into a pendant with a pin-to-pendant converter, a small metal attachment with a tube for the pin part, and a loop for your chain.

* A bangle bracelet that's too small for your wrist or a ring that's too big for your finger can take on new life hanging from a chain around your neck.

The above tips also offer a good DIY approach for things found in nature, such as shells with small holes in them, which can be strung on necklaces or hoop earrings.

BROOCH THE SUBJECT

Add an affordable, versatile, personal touch to your wedding-day outfit by pinning on a vintage brooch—anywhere you please. You can place it as an accent on your dress or sash (they can look particularly cool pinned to the back of a dress), use it to secure a shawl, or lash it to a comb and wear it in your hair for a bit of sparkle. Brooches also make great bridesmaids' gifts, and they can be incorporated into their outfits, too.

DIY Hair and Makeup

Who says you and the gals need full-on salon service? If no one in your party wants a complicated updo, then there's no reason that you can't do your own (or each other's) hair. Just have hot rollers and a couple of hot curling irons on hand, as well as a blow-dryer for do-overs.

If you're nervous about wading in to the wide world of cosmetology alone, tap a friend who always looks pulled together and polished. If she's willing to lead you on a makeup scouting-and-shopping expedition, test out a few looks and determine what supplies you need together. You could even ask her to do your and your brides-maids' makeup on the big day—just make sure you have all the necessary materials on hand, as well as a special thank-you gift for her.

Alternatively, visit a Sephora store or cosmetics counter for a makeover a few weeks before the wedding. (MAC has particularly creative, generous makeup artists, though you'll need to be clear about the look you're going for—or you could wind up wearing teal eye shadow.) You can include your bridesmaids and make it into a prewedding outing for the girls, or even your bachelorette party, if you're having one. Tell the makeup artist that you're working on a wedding-day look, and be upfront about likes, dislikes, and special requests. Note what products the artist uses and application tips he or she offers, and buy one or two products that you particularly like.

In general, your wedding-day makeup application should stick pretty close to your everyday routine—you don't want to look like anyone but your best self.

Beauty Tool Kit

Your groom wants to marry *you,* not an overly made-up imposter. However, on this monumental day, there are a few special products you might want to make sure you have in the bag:

* Waterproof mascara. It's a cliché, but just buy it.

* Clear brow gel. It makes brows look polished and natural.

* Clear, light pink, or peach lip gloss. Natural-looking lips are best when there's lots of kissing involved.

* Blotting papers. These are great for eradicating shine and dance-floor perspiration. Keep them tucked in your purse (and ask a trusted bridesmaid to alert you when you're looking a little shiny). You'll be happy when you get the photos back.

* A cake of bronzer and a big fluffy brush. In case you find yourself looking a little peaked, a bit of bronzer will restore a healthy glow.

* A tube of hydrocortisone cream. A little dab will help to soothe any small skin irritation and remove redness.

* Preservative-free lubricating eye drops. They'll make sure that your eyes look as bright and clear as possible.

* Preparation H or, for a more natural approach, chamomile tea bags. For banishing under-eye bags and puffiness.

* Lightweight hair spray. Even the most natural bride wants some hold on her wedding day.

* Anti-frizz serum. Essential for the taming of the 'do.

Now that you know what you need, here's what to do with it. Follow these tips and you'll create a complete look that's worthy of that gorgeous gown. Or is it the other way around?

* Do a full hair and makeup trial run the week before the wedding.

* If you're wearing eyeliner, don't line the lower lid—it will make your eyes look smaller in pictures.

* If you or the bridesmaids are exposing leg but forgoing stockings, consider using leg makeup. Grab a couple of cans of Sally Hansen Airbrush Legs in the appropriate shades. It's magic.

* Schedule your last round of beauty treatments—eyebrow wax, haircut, highlights, whatever—for one to two weeks before the wedding. That will leave that last week free of appointments, and it will also give you a little cushion to undo the results of a treatment gone awry. (Plus it leaves a little time for nature to take its course and soften everything up just a tad.)

* If you plan to get a series of facials leading up to the wedding, start early, and work with someone good. Watch your skin to see how it responds in the weeks following a treatment, and schedule your last facial accordingly.

* *Do not* introduce anything new to your beauty routine in the week before the wedding—not a mask, not a scrub, not a new shampoo or conditioner. If you're getting a massage, have the masseuse use a tried-and-true oil or lotion or something unscented. The last thing you want is an allergic reaction.

The Groom's Outfit

Poor old groom. Why is his default outfit always a rented tux and blindingly shiny shoes? Most grooms' outfits seem designed to fade into the background. And it seems especially tragic when you compare his fashion fate to all the attention lavished on the wear-it-once wedding dress. But it's his day, too, and a wedding is the perfect excuse to buy a well-cut (or even custom-made) suit. He'll wear it forever. But don't stop there. Why not mix it up, with bright ties, patterned vests, or suspenders? Any natty male accoutrement is fair game, as long as he loves it and it fits with the theme.

Consider these other options, suitable for the groom and all his groomsmen:

* For an outdoor wedding in the late summer or fall, casual luxury: dark jeans with a crisp white shirt or cashmere sweater and a blazer on top.

* For a beach wedding, Bahamian splendor: khaki shorts, white shirt, bright tie, and blue blazer.

* For a green wedding, natural elegance: a suit made from hemp fabric. (Hemp is ready to harvest about one hundred days after planting, making it one of the most sustainable crops around. To buy hemp fabric by the yard, check out www.greensage.com.)

* For a city wedding, urban sophistication: a slim dark suit with monochromatic shirt and tie.

* For a garden wedding in the late spring or early summer, a sense of humor: a seersucker suit with a bowtie (or no tie at all).

* For a spring or summer wedding: a tan or khaki suit with a pastel tie.

* For a period wedding: a vintage suit tailored to fit. (Pick something from the same era as your wedding dress.)

If you want to have a suit made, go to the best menswear shop in town, and ask who does their tailoring. Then find out if that operation does custom work. Brooks Brothers also has many made-to-measure options, and Nordstrom is tops among department stores, though you'll pay more if you go either of those routes. Some tailors may balk a little if you want to go with an unorthodox fabric like hemp, but you can charm them into working with you if you are very clear about your vision and listen to their recommendations about fabric requirements.

HOW TO MAKE CUSTOM CUFF LINKS

Cuff links are a classic, useful gift for the groom and his party, and they're a cinch to make. Here are two different approaches:

Option One: Buy cuff link backs, or "findings," with a 15mm flat surface at a craft or beading store or online (try www.inthecuff .com), or use an old pair of cuff links with a flat surface. Use epoxy or other strong glue (E6000 adhesive works well) to tack on a symbol of your love, such as a coin, a button, a sterling silver charm in any shape under the sun (see "Resources" on page 219 for Web sites that sell oodles of silver charms), a game piece from Monopoly or another board game, dice, Scrabble tiles in his initials—you get the picture.

Option Two: Tie any two objects together with a short cord or chain. For example, you could pair two vintage buttons, one bigger and showier (for the outside cuff), and one smaller and more discreet (for the inside cuff). Take a needle and a length of thick silk cord, and lace up the bigger button. Bring the thread out the back side of the button, and knot the cord firmly against it to push it flush. (A tool called a "knotter," designed for beading, can help you get the knot right where you want it.) Do not cut the cord. Loosely lace the cord through the hole of the smaller button. Pull the buttons toward each other, leaving roughly ⅓ inch of cord between them. Knot the thread against the back of the smaller button. To reinforce, repeat as many times as you like.

The Bridesmaids' Ensembles

News flash: *No one* wants to buy a dress she'll wear only once.
What's that? You knew that, but you forgot? Brides often do, no
matter how many one-night wonders are hanging in their own
closets. Or perhaps brides ask bridesmaids to buy matching dresses
precisely *because* of all those one-night wonders—it's payback time.

Or maybe it just seems too risky or bothersome to break with
tradition. But I'm here to tell you that you can skip the matchy-
matchy bridesmaid dresses *at no cost* to the aesthetics of your
wedding, and with no more effort than it would take to find that
one dress—which wouldn't look good on most of them anyway.
In fact, bridesmaids' dresses may be the easiest place to loosen
things up and incorporate a DIY touch.

Do Your 'Maids an Honor

To avoid the ten-girls-one-dress look, try the following:

* Begin by asking your 'maids, one by one, what they already have
  in their closets that might be suitable. Tell them when and where
  the wedding will take place, describe the setting in as much detail
  as possible, and mention any color decisions you've already made.
  One of them may own something that inspires the look of the
  whole wedding party.

* Inquire whether one or a couple of them would like to do the initial
  research—online, or in stores—on dresses and report back. Give
  them some rough guidelines and see what they come up with. This
  is a great strategy—you're doing less work, they feel involved, and
  you're drawing on more brains and creative spirits. It's a win-win.

* Ask each of them to wear a simply cut black or navy dress and buy
  (or make) them matching bracelets or necklaces. For a vintage look,
  try those fabulous multistrand plastic bead necklaces from the

fifties and sixties, or long strings of flapper beads to loop around the neck several times.

* Give them a color palette and free rein within it. You can give your instructions in many different ways, such as "a range of cool pinks, from light peony to raspberry," "anything in spring green and/or chocolate brown, in solids or patterns," or "the colors of hydrangeas—dresses in any light shade of blue or purple."

Tip: To firm up your color scheme, go to the hardware store and pull paint chips. Once you've got a suite of acceptable shades, make little color palettes for all your bridesmaids. If any of the wedding party members live far away, just slip their palettes into envelopes and drop them in the mail. ✑

If your bridesmaids choose their own dresses, ask each of them to check in with you before making a final decision. You can request that the bridesmaids share a digital photo with you and the rest of the group, if possible, so you can make sure that the scheme is building nicely with each addition. I used this approach, specifying "shades of pink and coral" and assembling the look woman by woman. Five of my seven bridesmaids wore something they already owned; the other two bought dresses that I hope they'll wear for a long time.

Whatever your approach, matching jewelry (the bolder the better), shawls, or other accessories can tie a look together—and don't underestimate the power of those matching bouquets to make them look like a group. If you want the flowers to be more integrated into their ensembles, consider getting corsages, or flowers for their hair, instead of bouquets. If you take that approach, make sure they have something else (like hankies, candles, or single flowers to add to an altar bouquet) to carry down the aisle. (It feels awkward to take that walk without something for your hands to do.)

One more thing—there's no need to ask your bridesmaids to wear matching shoes. No one will be looking at their feet. Seriously.

HOW TO EMBROIDER A HANKIE

A delicate handkerchief embroidered with initials or a symbol of the day makes a wonderful, old-fashioned keepsake for bridesmaids. (It's a sweet idea for the mothers of the bride and groom, too.) Wrap it around the stems of a bouquet or tuck it in a purse. You can also make masculine versions for the men in the wedding party.

MATERIALS:

- Pattern and materials for transfer (See step 1, below.)
- Hankie • Embroidery floss (I recommend DMC)
- Needle • Embroidery hoop, if desired

1. **Transfer your pattern to the hankie, using any of the methods listed here. Keep in mind that patterns or designs with clean, simple lines work best, and that the pattern probably should be applied to one corner of the hankie (see tip on the facing page).**

   ✳ Draw directly on the cloth with chalk or pencil, if you're a freestyle gal.

   ✳ Photocopy an image, and then trace over it with a transfer pencil (available at fabric stores). You can then transfer the image from paper to fabric with a hot iron—but be forewarned that any lettering will be backward, because the image is reversed.

   ✳ Pin dressmaker's carbon or tracing paper—available in red, blue, and white (the latter for use on dark fabrics)—on the hankie and place the pattern on top of it. Using a pencil, trace the outline on the paper and the image will transfer to the hankie.

   ✳ Trace an existing design onto tissue paper or tracing paper, and then pin the paper on the hanky in the desired place. You'll embroider over the paper, and carefully cut it away.

* The easiest way to go is to use a store-bought iron-on transfer pattern made with a special ink so they can be used more than once. Go to www.sublimestitching.com for a mind-boggling array of cool patterns.

2. **Using your embroidery floss and needle, embroider the design from the pattern onto the hankie. Solid stitching instructions abound on the Internet—again, try www.sublimestitching.com, or www.needlenthread.com, which includes instructional videos.**

A note on finding hankies: While men's handkerchiefs are everywhere, ladies' are a bit trickier to find, especially ones that aren't already adorned. Check linen, gift, and housewares stores in your area, or try www.giovannislinens.com or www.giftwagon.com.

Tip: If you wish, use photo transfer paper and an inkjet printer to transfer a color or black-and-white photo to the hankie. (Just follow the instructions on the package.) And, whether you're embroidering or using a photo, keep in mind that you want the image to be no larger than a quarter of the size of the fabric, so the image is neatly visible when the hankie is folded in quarters.

Bejewel Your Bridesmaids: Jewelry for Your Wedding Party

Perhaps the easiest bridesmaid gift and accessory is a simple necklace that you string together yourself, with bulk pearls or beads purchased at a bead shop. (If your city has a Chinatown, that's often the perfect place to get these materials on the cheap.) Get yourself a quick lesson in bead stringing from a friend in the know or from a professional; knotting between each bead using proper technique ensures that the piece comes out even and wears well. (See "Resources" on page 219 for how to find local options.)

Or customize a purchased necklace by adding a sterling silver charm that symbolizes the day—a sand dollar for a beach wedding, or a pinecone for nuptials in the forest—with a jump ring and needle-nose pliers, or even a tiny key-chain-style ring, which requires no tools. (For variety, attach the charm to the clasp of a necklace—a cool look for the back of the neck, especially for the bridesmaids who are wearing their hair up.)

Pearl stud earrings are also a breeze to make: Just buy "half-drilled pearls" (or any half-drilled bead you fancy) and posts; screw the special post head into the pearl and secure with a tiny dab of hot glue. You can even find posts for pearl clusters, with three-pronged heads.

Hang out in bead stores for inspiration and great advice—the people who work there are usually beaders themselves, and very knowledgeable.

HOW TO MAKE EASY CLUSTER EARRINGS

This is a perfect project for when you want something a bit fancier and more ambitious, but not so tedious that making multiple pairs would be a major chore. You can use any combination of three different beads, and play around with shades, shapes, and sizes until you find a pleasing arrangement. Or use the same kind of stone, in three different shapes. Do splurge on semiprecious stones and gold-filled hooks—your girls are worth it.

This design is courtesy of Ella Mei Yon Biggadike, a jewelry designer and friend who made a version of these earrings for my bridesmaids, who still wear them all the time.

MATERIALS:

• 2 main beads (Pick something robust enough to be the centerpiece of the arrangement.) • 2 complement beads (roughly one-half to one-quarter the size of your main bead)
• 6 accent beads (A stack of three accent beads should be roughly two-thirds the height of your complement bead.)
• A pair of gold-filled or 14-carat lever-back earring hooks (Don't bother with the gold-plated kind; they just won't last.)
• Needle-nose pliers • Gold-filled head pins (in the sizes that work for your beads) • Wire cutters

1. Lay all your beads out on a clean surface, under good light.

2. Gently open up the tiny loop at the bottom of the earring hook with your pliers. This is where you'll attach the beads.

3. Prepare the beads to be attached to the hooks by threading them onto the head pins. Slide the main bead on its head pin, and then set aside. Repeat this process with the complement beads, and, finally, with the stack of three accent beads. When finished, you should have three threaded head pins. Lay them all out, pointy-side up.

4. The main bead is what you'll attach to the hook's loop, via its head pin, and the other beads will hang off of the main bead's head pin like pendants, so prepare the smaller beads' head pins first. Start with the complement beads. Using the pliers, clamp on to the end of the head pin and bend it into a neat loop just above the top of the top bead. (For extra security, make the pin do one-and-a-half loops, rather than just one complete circle.) Trim off the extra with wire cutters. Slip the complement bead's loop on to the head pin of the main bead.

5. Repeat this process with the stack of accent beads, making a loop out of its head pin above the top bead and then slipping it on to the main bead's head pin, on top of the complement bead. You now have a little cluster of beads, ready to be attached to the earring hook as a single unit. You can use the pliers to manipulate the arrangement so it hangs to your satisfaction.

6. Now, make a loop out of the main bead's head pin as you did with the other head pins, and trim. Thread that loop into the loop on the bottom of the hook.

7. Close the hook's loop with pliers.

8. Repeat steps 4 through 7 for the other earring.

Deep Breath: Relax, Gorgeous

No matter what you wear, you're going to look stunning on your wedding day. The disheveled bride is statistically nonexistent. The same goes for your wedding party. Everyone will rise to the occasion. And people will look their absolute best if they're relaxed and unhurried—especially you. If there's anything you're making yourself, start early and work ahead, and have a backup plan in case things don't turn out. Keep your sense of humor. If you're worried about people having all their bits and pieces in line, make a checklist for them a couple of weeks before the wedding, and then try to stop worrying about everyone's attire. Just trust that it will all come together. Eat well: fruit, veggies, lean protein, and whole grains. Sleep as much as you can. Drink plenty of water. On the day of the wedding, give yourself plenty of time to get ready, more than you think you'll need. And breathe.

INVITATIONS
(and Other Ways to Spread the Word)
CHAPTER THREE

When it's time to get moving on paper products, you'd better round up that hubby-to-be and head out to the neighborhood stationery shop, right? Well, yes, if you're just looking for inspiration. But when it comes to making a purchase, maybe the stationery store is not quite the place for you. I'm all for shopping at small, locally owned businesses, because they deserve your support; they usually offer wonderful, personalized service, and they can often print up awesome, affordable custom creations, especially if they have an in-house designer. But when it comes to wedding invitations, let the buyer beware: many stores are hotbeds of giant corporate sample books and rampant up-selling, and it's hard to keep from getting sucked in. If you order your invitations through a certain kind of store, you could spend hours with the consultant poring over binders of invites, get hoodwinked into choosing embossed papers when you really couldn't give a hoot, and be fleeced in the end for $2,000 invites that look just like those from the last two weddings you attended (and, as a final indignity, that wind up in the trash, as all invitations do).

You know where I'm going with this: wedding invitations are a perfect place to DIY. You can save a ton of money, create something entirely personal and unique, and go easy on the environment at the same time, if you use recycled or wood-free paper and/or materials you already have on hand. Just keep in mind that what may look stunning (and seem doable) when you're working up a prototype

could be difficult to re-create in large quantities, or could start to look sloppy when fatigue and boredom set in after a few hours of repetitive assembly.

A GOLDEN RULE

No matter what level of DIY you choose for your invites, two caveats apply across the board:

1. Working backward from you RSVP deadline, build in plenty of time to get everything printed, assembled, and mailed.

2. Recruit lots of help.

Keep It Simple

Before you make design and printing decisions, think about the big picture. Of all of the pieces of a traditional formal invitation, how many do you really need?

At a minimum, the traditional invitation includes the following: an outer envelope, unsealed inner envelope, invitation, reception card, response card, response card envelope, and a map and/or directions.

That's not including the ubiquitous squares of tissue, a holdover from the days when the ink might have smeared, and newer items, such as folders to hold all the various components and fancy lined envelopes. How many of these could you live without? I can tell you right now that your guests won't miss tissue or inner envelopes, nor will they mind if you skip the response cards and envelopes and instead go with reply postcards, which will save postage money as well as trees. In fact, format is far less important than content: as long as you convey all the necessary info in warm, welcoming language, you'll have satisfied the rules of etiquette, and communicated effectively with your guests.

Here are the essentials:

* What (a wedding)
* Who (your names and possibly those of your parents, if they're helping to foot the bill)
* When (date and time)
* Where (venue, city, and state)
* How to RSVP
* How to get there (or the address of a Web site that will tell you how to get there)
* Reception time and place (if the ceremony and reception will be held at different locations)

Rest assured, even if your wedding is very formal, a simple invitation will suffice. You can set the tone through design and paper choice—and don't underestimate the power of the words "black tie."

Mistakes in printed material are a huge bummer, so proofreading is vital, and it's best done by someone (or two people, or three people) with fresh eyes. You can't be too careful.

When should you send your invitations? Opinions vary on this subject, but most experts would agree that six to eight weeks before the wedding will give guests plenty of time to plan their travel and clear their schedules, especially if you've sent a save-the-date card.

(If you want to save on postage, consider hand-delivering invitations to people you see frequently or who live near you.)

DRESSY CASUAL CHIC?

How do you communicate appropriate dress for your nuptials? I'm of the less-is-more school. I'd only specify one of three levels of dress formality on an invitation: white tie, black tie, or black-tie optional. Anything else—such as "rural chic" or "creative cocktail attire"—can come across as pushy, confusing, and way too cute. If the look of your invitations and wedding Web site sets the right tone, your guests will be smart enough to figure out what to wear—they're your friends and family members, after all.

More Invitation Tips

- Some Web sites sell custom invitation and envelope patterns and dies, if you really, really want to DIY, but most stationery shops have precut papers and envelopes in every shape and size.

- If you're purchasing envelopes rather than making your own, make sure everything fits smoothly inside them.

- Take the completed invitation with *all* its components to the post office and weigh it *before* purchasing postage.

- You can easily order personalized photo stamps online at www.stamps.com, though, sadly, you'll pay extra. But the post office always has at least two wedding-y stamp designs to choose from, along with plenty of nonwedding designs that might complement the personality of your event. (Go to www.usps.com to browse.)

- Put a return address on the main envelope, in case of mailing error.

- If you're considering hand-canceling your stamps in order to preserve the beauty of your envelopes, my advice is to spend your precious time on something else. I've heard of too many brides painstakingly canceling each piece of mail themselves (through a special arrangement with their local post office), and then seeing their invitations suffer anyway, stamped again by careless post-office staff or just generally chewed up in the mail. Spend more energy on what's inside the envelope.

- Be prepared for forgetful guests who might send back response cards without their names on them (it happens!) by assigning each guest a number and writing that number on the back of their response card with a pencil and a light hand. (This is easiest to do if you're keeping your guest list in a spreadsheet.) No one will notice the numbers, and you'll save yourself the trouble of tracking down the identity of any mysterious guests.

Invitation Options

The techniques described in this chapter can be adapted for use with any and all paper products—save-the-dates, invites, thank-you notes, place cards, programs—though specific program and thank-you ideas also appear in other chapters.

I've divided the projects into three levels of DIY difficulty:

* Simple—skip the stationery shop and hop online

* Moderate—find a graphic designer and/or printer

* Involved—DIY design, printing, and assembly

Simple: Skip the Stationery Shop and Hop Online

If you crave more flexibility and individuality than the giant sample books at stationery stores offer, but you don't want to do everything yourself, a great way to get DIY design without DIY labor is to assemble your invitations with the help of a Web site. This scenario means one-stop-shopping: choose your paper, font, design, and language, and have the cards shipped to you to assemble and mail. You don't need to hire a designer, find a printer, or get even a spot of ink on your hands, but you have more control over the design than you would when choosing a stock invite from a stationery store. This is a good option for DIYers who want a no-fuss, no-muss approach.

Here are some places to start Web-window shopping:

* The site www.mygatsby.com is out in front of the customizable invitation trend. They have tons of design options and zillions of colors and patterns.

* Another option, www.gartnerstudios.com, takes a tongue-in-cheek approach, with their www.brideasylum.com site, which urges you not to "let the invitations push you over the edge" and offers easy-to-create invitations that you can design online and print yourself.

* For a more classic look, www.aldengrace.com is also good. Its owners came from invitation giant William Arthur, a division of Hallmark, but their new company has a more indie sensibility. For example, they'll work with your custom art at no extra charge, something many Web sites won't do.

* Sites like www.youreinvited.net take a more collaborative approach, offering you access to an in-house designer who can create most anything you want.

* Photo sites provide lots of great options, too, if you have a stunning photograph—of the two of you, of the place where you're getting married, or of something else that's important to you—and want a more casual look.

Tip: *Even if you decide not to purchase your wedding invitations online, the sites listed can make good sources for rehearsal dinner or brunch invites.*

Moderate: Find a Graphic Designer and/or Printer

If you want something even more custom, it's remarkably easy to find a graphic designer who'll be willing to do a wedding-invitation project for a little extra cash. (Maybe you even have a friend who will design your invitations as a wedding present.) One girlfriend of mine didn't know any designers personally, so she posted an ad on a local design school's bulletin board and found a talented student. You could also call an advertising or marketing agency or any other business that has an in-house design staff to see if anyone there might be looking for extra work. When interviewing designers, be sure to ask to see a portfolio, and find out whether he or she has good contacts at printers before agreeing to do business together; you don't want to be left with a design that you're not sure how to print.

Creative Collaboration

Graphic designers put a lot of thought and feeling into their craft. Here are some tips for smooth sailing when working with the designer in your life:

- It's up to you whether you think a contract is necessary (see "Contracts 101" on page 214 for more info if you do). However, unless the designer insists on making his or her services a gift, it's wise to politely decline favors and attach money to the deal, even if it's just a token amount. Pay some up front, and the remainder on final delivery of the finished product. In the case of a gift, acknowledge the giver as you would acknowledge any member of the wedding party.

- Describe what you're looking for in as much detail as possible, and supply examples, if you can, to minimize confusion and decrease the number of drafts you have to go through before arriving at something that makes you happy. Speak his or her language: show pictures or describe visual details that evoke the feeling you're going for.

- Don't be surprised if creative differences arise. Use sensitivity when critiquing your designer's work, and be diplomatic when asking for revisions.

- Remember that you need to pay the designer *and* the printer. Make sure that you discuss whose responsibility it is to get quotes from printers (ideally, the designer will do this), and determine when in the design process this needs to occur.

- While you're still in the design phase, consider what elements you can live without in order to get the printing price you want. Do you really need more than one ink color? Can you skip the vellum? You don't want to wind up with a design that's prohibitively expensive to print and needs to be altered.

In Love with Letterpress?

A great way to give your invitations hand-crafted appeal is to seek out a small private press and have them letterpressed. Any design— including one you've drawn yourself—can be made into a custom-engraved letterpress plate and accented with metal type. For best results, you'll need to choose a soft paper that will really show the "bite" of the impressions, and costs may differ depending on whether you're using a standard ink or custom-mixed color. Yes, it's a bit finicky and labor intensive, but this process creates beautiful, textural results—and, because letterpress is an old craft that's had a loving renaissance of late, anyone who runs a letterpress is likely quite talented and enthusiastic and will help you create something really special. You may even be able to find local art students who would take on the design and/or printing of your invitation as a school project. (See "Resources" on page 220 for how to find letterpress printers in your area, or search online for "custom letterpress.")

Tip: Really dedicated DIYers might even want to do their own letterpress work— inexpensive letterpresses are available on eBay for under $250. Go to www.fiveroses.org for a very solid overview of the letterpress craft, plus information on how to get started if you'd like to DIY.

A Printing Primer

If you plan to hire a printer yourself, be ready to talk shop.

EMBOSSING AND DEBOSSING: With embossing, metal plates etched with letters are stamped into paper, so what is left behind is the raised imprint of the letter, like Braille. Debossing is simply the opposite: you're left with a lowered imprint of the letters. When there's no ink involved, it's called *blind embossing,* but ink can be added to make the embossed or debossed letters or images show up in color. This process creates beautiful borders, return addresses, and monograms.

ENGRAVING: Design and/or text is etched into a copper plate from a negative; the plate is inked and pressed into contact with paper, resulting in raised lettering on the front and "bruising" on the back of the paper.

LETTERPRESS: Letterpress is a relief printing method, with type or plates on which the areas to be printed are raised above the nonprinting areas. Ink rollers touch only the top surface of the raised areas; the nonprinting areas are lower and do not receive ink. The inked image is transferred directly to the page, resulting in images that may be debossed into the paper by the pressure of the press. Also called *block printing,* letterpress has a beautiful, handmade feel.

LITHOGRAPHY OR OFFSET AND DIGITAL: Though these are two different processes, the effect is the same. In offset printing or lithography, an inked impression on a plate or a rubber cylinder is transferred to paper. Ink colors are mixed in cans from Pantone or RGB colors for exact matches. With digital printing, a file is sent straight to a digital printer. The resulting images and text are flat, with no embossing or debossing—the kind of printing used for direct-mail postcards, posters, and so on.

THERMOGRAPHY: This method produces text that looks like engraved printing, but it's much cheaper. The process fuses ink and a resinlike powder together to make raised letters. Thermography can be used for type only.

Involved: DIY Design, Printing, and Assembly

I know one crafty couple who used a variety of techniques (collage, watercolor, calligraphy, stitching, and more) to make a unique, customized handcrafted invitation for each of the three hundred guests they invited to their wedding. No joke. They did it to save money, to take advantage of the luxury of their long engagement (almost two years), and to create a meaningful memento for their guests in lieu of traditional favors. But these two are also unusually ambitious. Luckily, there's a middle ground.

DIY Printmaking

If you're up for designing and printing your invitations entirely on your own, try rudimentary printmaking at home with linoleum blocks from an art store. You need one block for every color you want to print, as well as inks, a soft rubber roller or "brayer," and tools for carving your image into the block. (Linoleum cutters can be outfitted with various-size blades for more or less detailed work.) Printing text is tough with this technique, because the carved image needs to be very fine and the pressing done "just so" for the lettering to be legible, not to mention carved in reverse—you can always take the easy way and use a computer and printer for the text portion of your invitations; see "Desktop Designer" on page 86 for tips. But almost any image that's not too detailed can easily be transferred onto a block and printed, with the charming side benefit that no two prints come out exactly alike. (And you wouldn't be pursuing this path if you wanted carbon-copy perfection, right?) Just make sure to re-ink the block after each print, and to wash the block with warm water and dry it after every three or four prints. (Do a Web search for "block print" for more information.)

You can get more primitive still with a piece of Styrofoam, or even a vegetable—remember potato-block prints? If you like an organic, rough-hewn look, carve a simple shape into a potato (say, a conversation-heart shape with "WE DO" inside it for a Valentine's Day wedding, or a horseshoe for a Texas square dance) and stamp away. Or, for a reverse-print look, carve your design into a piece of Styrofoam (such as a thoroughly washed supermarket meat tray) with the point of a pencil, ink up the carved side with a roller, and press onto paper. Make sure to cut the Styrofoam into a pleasing shape, since the entire surface will be inked, and, again, remember that any lettering needs to be backward!

Desktop Designer

Perhaps the easiest and cleanest way to control the invitation production process from start to finish is to type up the text component using a word-processing program, and have it printed and cut into your desired shape at a copy shop (or use your own printer at home, and borrow a paper cutter elsewhere). Then just dress it up: attach it to a hand-printed background or a contrasting sheet of colored paper; wrap it with a ribbon; or adorn it with a decal, a scrapbooking cutout, or a rubber-stamped design (see "Stamping 101," on page 89). Read on for a few embellishment techniques.

THE EYELET

An eyelet is a great way to affix a printed piece of paper to a larger colored piece of paper with a little note of elegance. Plus, eyelets come in tons of colors and shapes, so you can coordinate them with other wedding accessories.

To use eyelets, you need a scrapbooking hole punch, an eyelet setter, and a hammer. (I'll give full instructions here, because I used this approach for my wedding programs and, frustratingly, found that the tools' packaging contained no instructions.)

Working atop a self-healing mat or an old magazine to protect your table or countertop, make a small pencil mark where you want the eyelet to go, place the tip of the hole punch on the mark you made, and plonk it with the hammer. Place the eyelet in the hole, through the front of your invitation. Flip the papers over so you are looking at the back, making sure that the eyelet stays in place. Put your eyelet setter on the back of the eyelet. Whack the eyelet setter with the hammer until the eyelet ends split and flatten out, holding the papers together. Experiment with force and number of hammer whacks. To attach the papers more securely, fortify with a glue stick or spray adhesive.

THE WRAP AND TIE

A decorative sleeve wrapped around a printed piece is a delicate, pretty way to dress up a simple invitation, and a useful way to hold multiple pieces of paper together in a package. Cut a strip of lightweight, decorative paper (wrapping or origami paper is ideal) to the desired size, minding how much overlap you want. Use a bone folder to make a very sharp crease on each side, as if the invitation were a

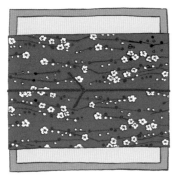

package and the sleeve were wrapping paper. Fold one edge over another; you can put the overlap on the front of the invitation or the back, depending on the look you want to achieve. Hold it in place with a decal, sealing wax, raffia, twine, or very fine ribbon.

THE PUNCH AND TIE

Use a hole punch to penetrate two pieces of paper at the same time, and then thread a fine ribbon or raffia through and tie firmly to hold the papers together.

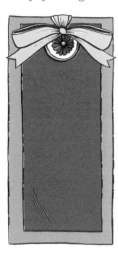

There are two different ways to do it:

(a) punch two small holes side by side, any distance apart, and thread the ribbon or raffia from back to front so you can tie a bow in front, or

(b) punch one larger hole, near the top of the papers, and thread the ribbon or raffia through it in a vertical loop.

Keep the desired technique and width of ribbon in mind when you purchase your hole punch, because they come in different sizes. Finish with a knot or bow. You can also attach a small charm, paper cutout, or tag to the ribbon at the same time.

Stamping 101

Rubber stamps are easy, efficient tools for creating custom looks and DIY details. The variety of stamps and inks out there is mind-boggling and there are Web sites that create stamps in any design you like. (See "Resources" on page 221 for ideas on where to buy.) You can also use old "hot type" or moveable type letters (made for use with old printing presses; look in antique stores) with an ink pad—they make a rough, artsy imprint, because the stamp doesn't absorb the ink evenly.

And if you adopt just one suggestion from this book, let it be this: Get yourself a stamp or embosser with your names and address on it. It's an invaluable tool for creating DIY invitations. You can use it for the return address on the main envelope; the address on the front of the reply envelope, if you use one; and again when you send thank-you notes.

If you want to fancy up your rubber-stamping technique, try embossing powder, which adds dimension to paper products with hardly any extra weight. Just stamp your design using glycerin (if you plan to use colored embossing powder) or a thick coat of colored stamp-pad ink (if you'll be using clear embossing powder). While the stamp is still wet, sprinkle embossing powder onto the stamped portion, then pour off the excess. Use a hair dryer to heat up and solidify the embossing powder to complete the embossed design.

Paper Tools

A few handy tools open up a wide world of design possibilities:

- Bone folder: This tool makes razor-sharp creases.

- Cutting mat or self-healing mat: You can use a thick magazine instead, but if you're doing a lot of work it makes sense to invest in a mat to save your surfaces.

- Eyelet setter: This handy tool attaches papers to one another with an eyelet, adding a clean-looking decorative element to your invitations or other printed materials.

- Foam double-stick tape: Use it to attach an element to a page and raise it up at the same time, creating a 3-D effect.

- Hole punch: You now can find them in every shape under the sun, but the ones that make round holes work best.

- Mini paper cutter: As long as your paper isn't terribly thick, these work beautifully, and spare you trips to Kinko's.

- Scalloped-edge scissors or pinking shears: These fancy-edge scissors are perfect for creating decorative borders.

- Seals and wax: Hot wax pressed with a seal imprinted with an initial or icon looks old-fashioned and elegant—but don't use this as a technique for outer envelopes that will go through the mail. The wax won't hold up to postal handling.

- Spray mount: An aerosol glue; it sprays on in a smooth layer, with no bulk or bunching. Use in a well-ventilated area.

- X-ACTO knife or retractable blade: This cutting tool is vastly superior to scissors for many tasks. It makes clean cuts and is very sharp! Use care.

Reproducing Images

If you have an image, such as a drawing or a photograph, that you'd like to incorporate into your invitation design in some fashion, it's easy to scan it and manipulate it in a design program.

Alternatively, you can try to get your hands on an opaque projector (buy one for less than $150, or work all your teacher connections and borrow one from a local school). These work like the overhead projectors we all remember from our school days, except that they will project any photograph, image from a book, or other opaque, flat object—the image doesn't need to be printed on a transparency. Opaque projectors work beautifully when you want to reproduce or enlarge images, but, because you'll be doing the tracing, simple designs are best unless you have a very steady hand. The projector shines a bright lamp onto the object from above, and a system of mirrors, prisms, and/or imaging lenses focuses the image onto a viewing screen or a wall. Tape up a piece of paper on the wall, project the image on top of that, and trace away.

Be aware that the image you are reproducing may be protected by copyright. Chances are you'll never get caught if it's only for personal use (and, ethically, it's probably OK, but only you can decide whether your conscience bothers you). But if you're distributing the invitation extremely widely for some reason, seek permission.

Easy Save-the-Dates

A postcard is the perfect vehicle for sending advance news of your wedding. Plus, you'll spend less on postage than you would with a card and envelope. You can have something designed and/or printed up, or simply buy postcards you like. A scenic shot of the wedding location is a wonderful way to whet your guests' appetites. Troll flea markets or eBay to get the friendly, kitschy tone of vintage postcards. If you're lucky, you'll find a whole bunch related to your location or theme. (Remember, there's no reason they all have to match!)

To print the information your guests need on the back of the post-cards, have a copy shop print them for you, or do it yourself using Microsoft Word and clear laser address labels (1 by 2⅝ inches). In the "Envelopes and Labels" dialogue box (under "Tools" and "Letters and Mailings"), click the "Labels" tab, type your information in the field, choose "Full page of the same label," and then "Print." Three of these labels stacked on top of one another fit quite well in the designated writing space on a standard-sized postcard.

This method works especially well if you are creating a wedding Web site. In that case, all you need are a few joyous words—"We're getting hitched!"—the date, the Web site address, and the promise of an invitation to follow. Guests can then visit your Web site to get information on travel arrangements and lodging.

You can also e-mail your save-the-date, though you'll also need to have a plan for communicating with people who either don't have an e-mail account or don't check it often. For these guests, a phone call or a short note on ordinary stationery could work fine.

If you plan to e-mail your announcement, give it some extra person-ality with a graphic component, be it an HTML e-mail, a jpeg, or a PDF attachment. An HTML e-mail is simply a static Web page that gets sent in a special way so the receivers' programs know to display it as a picture—if their settings are saved just so. But that's only one of many potential problems with sending and receiving HTML e-mails. A jpeg or a PDF attachment is the safer way to go; because they're effectively a "photograph" of a document, they ensure that everyone sees exactly the same thing when they open the attachment. Anyone with some graphic design skills can create a jpeg, and most computer programs have an easy way to turn a document into a PDF that can be attached to a group e-mail. On the other hand, some people have trouble opening attachments, so an e-mailed save-the-date is generally best for a younger, tech-savvy crowd.

Be Green

Invitations generate mammoth amounts of waste. Here are some ways you can reduce your environmental impact:

- E-mail your save-the-date, and create a robust wedding Web site with travel information and directions (this reduces the amount of paper you need to mail your guests). Consider using an electronic RSVP form on your site instead of asking people to respond via snail mail.

- If you're unsure about going digital, use postcards (rather than cards with envelopes) whenever you can, specifically for save-the-dates and RSVP cards.

- Does everyone need a save-the-date? Do you need to send them at all? Consider sending them only to people with whom you don't communicate on a regular basis, or skipping them altogether. In any case, limit the save-the-date list to people you will definitely be inviting to the wedding! There's no rule that says you have to send save-the-dates to every guest, but if you do send someone a save-the-date, then you must follow up with an official invitation.

- Skip inner envelopes and tissue paper.

- Choose 100-percent recycled or wood-free paper. The site www .organicweddings.com sells tree-free (made from quick-growing organic material) and recycled paper specifically for wedding invitations, and they'll send you free samples so you can make sure you like the way the paper looks. If you want more background on recycled and tree-free paper, check out www.conservatree.org.

- Choose an environmentally conscious printer. If you're not hiring the printer yourself, communicate your wishes to whoever is in charge of this task. Try www.ecoprint.com, www.greenerprinter .com, or www.rollingpress.com.

- See what you have on hand. Paper? Fabric? Ribbon? You may already have some great invitation materials in your possession.

The Wedding Web Site

I'm a huge fan of the minimal invitation and maximized Web site model. I'd even be in favor of entirely digital invitations for certain casual weddings, if I weren't so hopelessly devoted to paper products. But no matter how you invite your guests, a clean, well-organized Web site is a great companion to your invitation, and an invaluable help to guests as they plan their travel, pack for your event, and buy you gifts (etiquette prohibits putting registry information on the actual invitation, and I agree with that rule, but I don't think it's tacky to put it on your site). Many companies specialize in creating wedding Web sites (see "Resources" on page 221 for a list to get you started), but for my wedding, I took a more DIY approach (surprise!).

Here's why: marketing. We wanted to pick a domain name that people would remember without having to glance back at the save-the-date card, or the invitation insert (which many of them would probably misplace, anyway). We wanted something that would stick in our guests' heads the first time they saw it and thus would make it easy for them to call up our wedding details anytime they went online, anywhere in the world. (How many times have you found yourself wanting to look up the details of someone's wedding and wondered, "Was it www.sonnyandcher.com? Cherandsonny.com? Sonny-Cher.com?")

You can sidestep that issue with a one-of-a-kind URL. We chose www.nebraskanuptials.com, and it never failed to get a chuckle. And not once did anyone ask me, "What was your wedding Web site, again?" Go to a site such as www.networksolutions.com to see what's available, secure the domain name, and utilize their hosting services. Many hosting sites offer design services, too, though of course you can have anyone design the site.

Deep Breath: Signed, Sealed, Delivered

Until the wedding day, the invitations are for your guests. After that, however, they'll be for you. The way they look, read, and feel should bring you pleasure—it's your scrapbook they'll end up in.

Because your invitations are a communication tool, they should say something about the way you want your wedding day to be. For guests who pay attention to these sorts of things (read: females and gay men), the look and feel of the invites will give a first impression of your nuptials and begin to set the tone of the event. So, of course you'll want to put some thought and energy into them, and you don't want to neglect any basic information. But you're the boss here—if you love stationery, do it up; if you'd rather spend energy elsewhere, keep it super-simple. When you're happy with whatever you've created, it's good to go.

Try not to overconcern yourself with etiquette or rules, as politicized as the invitation debate may become, particularly where wording is concerned. The bottom line: make sure the language makes you and your fiancé happy, and that it works for either or both sets of parents, if they're mentioned. Give anyone whose name appears on the invitation the courtesy of reviewing the invitation and weighing in. Politely tell anyone whose name doesn't appear on it to pipe down. Make the final call yourselves. And breathe.

PHOTOS
AND VIDEO
CHAPTER FOUR

Great wedding photography doesn't just capture the essence of the day. It also captures the essence of your relationship, your feelings for one another, and your affection for your guests (and vice versa). It's impossible to take your own photos, of course—you'll be in front of the lens, not behind it—but you can DIY by choosing a photographer who shares your vision, using all the amateur resources in your stable, and setting up ways for guests to capture their own images.

The photos—and video, should you choose to have one—really will endure longer than anything else from the wedding, and thus they deserve plenty of your time and attention in the planning process. The best way to get brilliant results is to work all the angles: recruit several helpers, and choose two or three of the various techniques described in this chapter.

And here's the bottom line: if anyone offers to take pictures of your wedding, tell them to go for it! If you make it a collective effort, you'll wind up with wonderful images in a variety of formats and styles—an eclectic collection of memories that preserves all the different moods a wedding can evoke.

DIY Photography

Hiring a "Nonwedding" Photographer

Traditionally, wedding photographers made portraits and friends and family took care of the candids. That's changing, as more and more brides and grooms want photojournalism-style shots, or images of their big day that look more like fashion or art photography. The great news is that, when you look beyond the territory of wedding photographers, you'll find a world of options. If you have a family member or close friend who's a good photographer, then half your work is done. (See below for tips on dealing with that unique situation.) If you aren't so lucky, start looking for help in all the *un*usual places: Are there colleges near you, especially visual arts, photography, or film schools? You can post a notice on a bulletin board on campus or online to see if that shakes out any candidates. This is a great way for students to build their portfolios, so you may find a really talented photographer for a song. Ditto for your local newspaper—call the photo desk and ask if anyone does weddings. You may find your man or woman on the first try.

Hiring a Friend or Relative

Hiring a talented friend or family member may require a delicate touch. Choose your approach based on whether the person in question would be invited to the wedding even if you didn't want his or her services. Photographing a wedding is hard work. And if this is someone you'd be inviting anyway, and you're asking him to shoot your wedding, then he'll be working hard instead of enjoying leisurely vodka tonics and canapés, and you should acknowledge as much ("We'd love for you to shoot our wedding, but only if it would add to your enjoyment of the event").

Carefully gauge the person's response. If he seems genuinely interested in participating, say, "What can we do to make sure that you have plenty of time to relax and have fun too?" That may mean giving your photographer an hour or two off duty to eat and socialize while someone subs in, or hiring or assigning an assistant. Make it clear that you'll pay for film, processing, and any other costs. When he agrees to participate, send a handwritten note of thanks. On the wedding day, give a token of your appreciation.

If you're interested in procuring the services of a friend or business contact who didn't make the guest list, proceed differently. How well you know this person will influence how awkward it might be for him to walk the line between invited guest and vendor. If this photographer doesn't want to do it, we can hope that he will just say no.

Either way, if he agrees to the gig, make sure to do the following:

* Pay for the photographer's transportation to the event, and a hotel room, if an overnight stay is necessary.

* Make sure that he or she feels cared for—assign someone to supply food, drinks, and cake.

* If you're doing a sit-down dinner, make sure your photographer has a seat, and, if you're not, make sure there's a quiet, safe spot for stashing equipment and taking breaks. It will be appreciated, even if it's not used much.

* Hire or appoint a photo assistant.

* Pay for film and processing, if necessary.

Questions to Ask a Photographer

Determine his or her availability and consider asking:

- "How many weddings have you shot?"

- "May I see your portfolio?"

- "Who are some of your favorite photographers?"

- "What would you charge to shoot our wedding?" (Try to get the photographer to throw out a number first, rather than telling him or her your budget up front—but do go into the meeting knowing the upper limit of what you have to spend.)

- "What kind of camera do you use? Would you shoot digital or film?" (If film, ask about color, black-and-white, or both.)

- "Do you have a backup camera, or access to one?"

- "Do you have an assistant, or can you hire one for the day? Would there be any charge for him/her? Would it be OK if we appointed a guest to be your assistant for the evening?"

- "If you are going to print us a stack of proofs, can we keep them? Can we get a disk with all our images on it, or buy the negatives? If not, will you charge us per print?"

- "Do you have access to an online photo-viewing service, such as Pictage (www.pictage.com) so we can view our proofs online?"

In general, try to suss out whether your styles match—that's a pretty big deal. You and your photographer should have similar opinions on how posed or natural you want the photos to be. And note that any solo (or lead) photographer needs an assistant, whether it's the photographer's usual partner or someone you nab from your inner circle. It's just too difficult to manage without one.

When you've found a strong candidate, turn to "Contracts 101" on page 214 for help with writing up an agreement.

Equipment

If you've got the photographer, but he doesn't have the equipment, below is a bare-minimum list of what you'll need to provide, by either borrowing or renting.

- Camera
- Backup camera
- Flashes
- Tripod
- Assistant
- List of shots you want (consider www.theknot.com's photo checklist.)

Setting Up a Round Robin

If you can't find—or don't want—a single (professional or amateur) photographer to capture the wedding day from start to finish, or you just want more coverage, consider creating a friends-and-family photographer roster, with everyone taking a shift. Make sure you have a high-quality digital camera, along with a gigantic memory card (or two, or three) and a backup battery, available for their use. Make a list of the best photographers among your guests. Break the event up into shifts (ceremony, reception until dinner, dancing, and the like—whatever makes the most sense for your event) and assign two people—a photographer, and a buddy/assistant/drink fetcher—per shift. Make it the responsibility of each photographer to hand equipment off to the next, but make sure a reliable bridesmaid or groomsman knows the roster, just in case.

Photographers should be notified if anything big (such as the cake cutting or bouquet toss) is scheduled to happen during their shift, so they don't get distracted shooting the ring bearer stealing maraschino cherries from the bar and miss it. (Another tip: Put anyone who likes to booze on an early shift.) Because it's not a full-time job, you shouldn't have trouble getting people excited about volunteering. They'll likely be flattered that you asked, and they will enjoy the excuse to be near the celebs of the day.

Even if you don't set up a roster, encourage your friends to bring cameras and snap away. You'll be grateful for their shots—someone who knows you will know what to look for and may wind up capturing better moments than a stranger ever could.

"Prom" Photos, Polaroids, and More!

Once you know you've got the basics covered, it's time for some fun photo add-ons.

"Prom" Photos

Remember your prom photos? That fake arbor, those sparkly lights, maybe a slogan emblazoned on a banner behind you. No matter the setting, the result is the same: put up a backdrop, and people instinctively begin to pose. In the world of red-carpet photography, this phenomenon is called a "step-and-repeat," because the beautiful people swarm by in an endless stream while the shutters pop like firecrackers. Whatever you call it, a station set up with a portrait background (yes, sort of like the photo studio at Sears) and a camera can capture some priceless moments.

Almost anything can serve as a background. Below are some ideas:

* Scout around for a visually appealing surface somewhere in or around your reception space, such as a brick wall, cool wallpaper, heavy curtains, or a garden wall covered in ivy.

* A red carpet step-and-repeat background usually has a sponsor logo on it, so why not take the same approach and put in a plug for your wedding? Locate some clean, blank wall space and stick

up custom vinyl lettering with your names and the date, or use stencils to decorate a bedsheet or drop cloth with letters and/or designs. (See Chapter Ten and "Resources" on page 225 for sources.)

* Ask your photographer if he or she has access to a muslin backdrop, or rent one from a photography supply store.

* For a kitschier approach, you might hire a local sign company to print inexpensive banners of the kind that you really might have had behind you at your prom.

You can either assign a guest to man the camera, or set it up as a self-service station—you may get funnier shots that way. As an alternative, you can even rent a real photo booth from a party supply company. It could set you back around $1,000, but it would make for great, easy favors for your guests. (See "Resources" on page 222 for how to find a photo booth vendor.)

Assign someone to keep one eye on the photo station to make sure everything is going well. Put a digital camera on a tripod and attach a bulb, or print up step-by-step instructions on how to use the camera's self-timer. You can send the shots to people later, either attached to an e-mail or in the form of a printed photo card ordered from an online photo service.

A variation on this theme is to assign someone (a wedding-party member, perhaps) to snap pictures of guests when they come out of the receiving line. Alternatively, try a manned "photo guest book" station. You can even encourage tomfoolery with the help of a choice prop or two—hats, masks, or anything else that's in keeping with the mood of the event.

"WE DID" Advice From Real Couples

"We got married in Vegas, and, instead of having a traditional guest book, we had a life-size cardboard cutout of Elvis. Instead of signing in, guests were asked to pose with Elvis while my bridesmaids took pictures. Now we have all the photos of our guests hamming it up, which can be put into a nice photo album (which I'm embarrassed to say we haven't actually done yet). I think it's an idea that could work at other venues: if you were on the beach, guests could pose next to a tiki torch or palm tree; at a New York wedding you could have a cheesy cutout of the Brooklyn Bridge or Statue of Liberty."

—**Lara Corey, San Francisco, on her Sin City nuptials**

Don't Dis the Polaroids

It's a fact—everyone loves instant cameras. They love them so much, that if you have them at your wedding you should buy double the amount of film you think you'll need, because people will take at least half of the shots home. (Preempt that behavior by making the pictures your favors—just print up stickers with your names, the date, and any message you desire for people to slap on the bottom of the photos.)

Set up a Polaroid station with one or several cameras, or you could place a Polaroid camera in the "prom photo" setting described on page 102. Include clear instructions in large type regarding what you would like your guests to do. ("Please leave the cameras here," "Please circulate with the cameras," "Please display your photos on the bulletin board to your left," "Please take the photos home with you and enjoy"—whatever you like.)

Polaroids also make for a fun, casual photo guest book that's created on the spot. Have a guest book attendant snap the Polaroids and tape 'em into the book, and ask the guests to sign next to their picture.

Large Group Photos

A photo that includes everyone at your wedding makes a fabulous keepsake. Here are some tips for shooting everyone in one fell swoop:

* Scope out the location of your shot beforehand—the dance floor is often a good choice.

* Decide when you'll take the shot. The end of the reception may make for more interesting shots, but you'll be missing the folks who went to bed early.

* Give the DJ or emcee a heads-up that you'll want to gather everyone for a group photo, and an estimate of when you'll do it, so she can make the announcement when you give the signal.

* Have a stepladder or chair on hand, in case that nets a better angle (and have someone to steady the chair for the photographer).

* Take multiple photos as quickly as you can. You may want to shoot some before everyone is ready, for candid effect.

* Make the bride and groom the focal point, of course. Get some shots of everyone looking at the camera, and some of everyone looking at the couple of the hour.

"Say Cheese," and Other Avoidable Clichés

Don't bother with the disposable cameras at every table. They take terrible pictures even without user error, and there can be a lot of user error when people are drinking as much as they tend to at weddings. Some of the cameras will inevitably "walk away" or get lost, and you'll have wasted money both on the cameras themselves and on the processing.

But, in general, *do* circulate and get a shot of you and the spouse with every table, if you're having a sit-down meal. Have your photographer shadow you and snap away as you move from one table to the next. That way you'll know you've got a picture of everybody, and all of your guests will feel that you cared enough to take the time to capture a photo with them. While you're at it, spend a little time chatting with the guests at each table. This tactic not only provides a brilliant alternative to a receiving line but can also help to control traffic at the buffet, if you wrap up your chat at each table with an invitation to line up for food. Just make sure you, the groom, or your DJ or emcee makes an announcement beforehand, so guests know what's happening.

DIY Video

It may seem corny to videotape your wedding, but most brides and grooms who do it are glad they did. It's also one of the few things that really are best left to a professional or a very talented amateur friend. (It's not just the shooting that's tricky—the editing is equally challenging.) However, you *can* find people with camera skills who won't charge an arm and a leg—try advertising at local colleges with video and film departments. Or get really creative: one couple I know found their videographer through the groom's brother, a high school baseball coach who has the guy record all his games.

There are ways to capture your wedding on video without professional help. For example, if you want a retro look, consider purchasing a Super 8 camera on eBay. Or set up a video station in a corner, with the camera on a tripod, for people to stop by and record their thoughts about the just-married couple. Set up at least two chairs, a loveseat, or a bench in front of the camera. (Remember the couples' vignettes in *When Harry Met Sally?*) Or you can send someone around with a handheld recorder and ask people to talk about the two of you and their thoughts about the day. (You could do the same thing with a handheld tape recorder or digital audio recorder, for simplicity's sake.)

If you do ask a friend or family member to record the ceremony and high points of the reception, make sure the appointed person uses the best equipment available, and a tripod. For taping your ceremony, suggest that the volunteer get as close to the two of you as possible—the less zooming, the smoother the shot.

Deep Breath: Freeze Frame

It **is** important to document your wedding. The photos will likely last longer than anything else from the big day. But, with more digital cameras and amateur shutterbugs around than ever before, you'll certainly have some great keepsakes even if you skip a "real" photographer altogether. (We received six or seven separate batches of digital photos from guests after our wedding, and each batch had some superb shots.) So resist the temptation to blow your budget, and try to keep any photography-related crises in perspective.

Also remember that photos are not the only way to remember your wedding and preserve those memories for posterity. Writing a heartfelt pre-ceremony note to the guy who'll be standing at the end of the aisle is like taking a snapshot of your emotions. If you keep a journal regularly, try to make time to jot down a few entries in the weeks and days before the wedding, no matter how busy things get, and to record your impressions the day after. At the very least, do a big download during your honeymoon. If you don't keep a journal, consider starting one—it's a fabulous way to deal with engagement stress. And breathe.

FOOD AND DRINK

CHAPTER FIVE

Think it's crazy to try to cater your own wedding? It's definitely not for everyone, but you *can* pull off a menu of DIY delicacies—if you have plenty of help, if you're willing to redefine what you think of as "wedding food," and especially if you have a smaller guest list. And even if you want to leave this area to the professionals, there are lots of DIY tips, tricks, and touches that will ensure you get exactly what you have in mind.

Contrary to what wedding magazines might have you think, the sit-down dinner, with its multiple courses and waitstaff tripping over one another, is far from mandatory. In fact, it can be pretty far from ideal: It's expensive, it often results in cold entrees, and it discourages mingling. Actually, a full meal of any kind isn't a prerequisite. Perhaps you want to reserve a full sit-down meal for a more intimate rehearsal dinner. Whatever you serve, make it something you personally love to eat. Just be sure that you tell your guests what to expect—such as "light brunch following the ceremony," "cocktails and hors d'oeuvres," or "buffet supper and dancing"—on the invitation.

DIY Food

On the big day, any carefully edited selection of delicious food and drink that fits the setting and spirit of your event—in ample

quantities—can't fail. Here's another instance where it's helpful to think about your wedding as you would any other party. Make the food a natural extension of the place you're getting married, the time of year, and the time of day. Make it seasonal, fresh, and simple.

Do keep in mind, though, that party food is tricky. It's hard to prepare fresh, great-tasting food for a lot of people and serve it to every one of them at peak quality. And you can stress yourself silly trying to appeal to guests' diverse tastes. Further, the place where you're having the reception may have more food rules than a Jenny Craig convention. If you choose a venue with catering built in, it's unlikely that they'll let you provide your own eats, or use anyone else's services, except perhaps for your cake. However, if you're getting married someplace without endless rules or restrictions, your field of possibilities is much wider—which is more daunting, and also more exciting. Let's dig in.

"WE DID" Advice From Real Couples

"We had a champagne-and-cake reception on the lawn of my husband's family's church. I didn't like the idea of a long, five- to six-hour reception, so we kept it simple and just had gorgeous flowers, excellent champagne, and cake from the best French bakery in town. We both liked the old-fashioned idea of leaving for your honeymoon straight from the wedding and reception, so that's what we did. We toasted and mingled with our guests for about two hours, and then Matt and I changed in the church and said our good-byes. I tossed my bouquet to the girls as the jazz band played 'What a Wonderful World.' A limo—with our bags already in the trunk—took us to the airport to board our honeymoon flight to Tuscany. It was just the perfect day, and most important, I think it really reflected us as a couple and individuals. We planned the details to be the best quality available, but we chose what to focus on, and kept it simple. And it was really fun to arrive in Florence the morning after our wedding in my 'going-away suit' with my hair still done up from the wedding."

—Holly Hanisian, on her Cincinnati, Ohio, wedding to husband Matt

Sit-Down Dinner Alternatives

All Hail the Buffet

If you do decide to serve a full meal, the buffet is the DIY bride's best friend. It imparts a sense of bounty and festivity that appeals to the kid inside of most of us. Plus, timing is much less of an issue, and your need for serving staff is drastically reduced. Consider setting out a spread that includes any of the following:

* Green salad, with multitudes of toppings, and other vegetable salads and dishes

* Gourmet hot dogs, sausages, and burgers (turkey, beef, and veggie), served with every kind of cheese and condiment imaginable

* Sundae fixings, with ice creams, sorbets, fruit, nuts, and hot and cold toppings

* An assortment of meats that are good at room temperature— carved roast beef and a side of salmon, for example—with a variety of sauces

* A brunch buffet, with a hot egg casserole, carved ham and turkey breast, salads, and baked pasta dishes

Get Pot-Lucky

For extremely casual weddings, consider a main-dish potluck— seriously! You can ask guests to bring their specialties in lieu of wedding gifts. Or make a potluck buffet one component of the total spread. I know one bride with a big Italian family who plans to do that with a dessert buffet: She'll add a line on the reply card asking if the guest would like to contribute a treat for the dessert table, and requesting that he or she write in the name of the dessert. Then she'll make up cards to mark each dish, so when guests stop by the dessert table they'll know if they're sampling "Aunt Ana's Pizzelles" or "Cousin Gina's Almond Brittle."

Takeout

For an easy DIY road to lots of variety, consider assembling a meal from cheap ethnic takeout. You can get dumplings, hot wings, spring or summer rolls, cold sesame noodles, pierogi, sushi rolls, and pretty much anything else you can think of from an assortment of local vendors. You could stick to one ethnicity, or mix it up, as you would with the various "stations" (pasta, sushi, and so on) an expensive caterer might try to sell you. If you're using a variety of vendors, no one vendor should get too overloaded or stressed out, and the quality should stay consistently high. This approach is ideal for couples who are adventurous ethnic eaters by nature, with like-minded friends, and it's a great way to showcase the best local cuisine.

The key to making this look deliberate rather than haphazard is plenty of variety, and larger quantities. Zero in on the places you love to eat and scan their menus for sturdy items that will hold up during the big feast. Then call up the restaurant and tell them what you have in mind, discussing quantity, price, timing, and any special requests you might have regarding dishes (for example, chicken must be cut up into bite-size pieces). You should be able to schedule the food delivery to the reception site with near pinpoint accuracy, so just have pretty serving dishes ready and plenty of helpers on hand to get things loaded up, and perhaps access to a microwave in case something needs reheating.

Boxed Lunch or Dinner

Boxed picnic meals add a rustic, old-fashioned feel to an outdoorsy wedding. To take the stress out of serving, have helpers make up picnic meals the morning of the wedding. Choose items that hold up well—fruit, cheese, crackers, sandwiches, fried chicken, hard-boiled eggs, sturdy brownies—and package them in boxes or brown bags with napkins and cutlery. (Unbleached waxed paper bags make attractive, environmentally friendly single serving packages.)

Simple embellishments make all the difference. Tie up a napkin-and-cutlery bundle, main dish, and/or the box or bag itself with ribbon or raffia. Place a fresh flower inside the box. Put a personal "place card" on each box or bag, or write guests' names directly on the packaging in a creative way. Building in a short walk from the boxed-lunch table to the dining spot adds to the sense of adventure. Add a bar with cold drinks and you're good to go.

Delicious Little Meals

Here are some location-specific serving suggestions that can help you circumvent the sit-down dinner without sacrificing style:

- On a sunny patio with a stunning view: a simple brunch and champagne cocktails

- In a loft or the cool marble lobby of an elegant building: light hors d'oeuvres and a martini bar

- In a cozy library full of leather furniture: a dessert buffet, with coffee and liqueurs

- At a private home, or in the courtyard of a pretty little church: cake and punch

- In a vineyard setting: a wine tasting with fruit and cheese

- On an enclosed patio strung with twinkling lights: guacamole, chips, and margaritas

Negotiating with Your Caterer

If you decide to work with a restaurant or caterer but feel boxed in by the packaged options, speak up. Many times the menus they present are just samples to simplify things and help speed overwhelmed brides and grooms toward a decision. In fact, your caterer might be happy to help you add to, subtract from, or break down those monolithic packages into something that's more "you."

* After you've studied the sample menus, focus on the items you like and would consider ordering. Express a desire to explore using them as part of a custom menu.

* Ask whether your caterers are willing to use family recipes, if there's a particular dish you'd really like to serve.

* Ask if you can meet with or speak directly to the chef. Much of the time you'll be working through an event planner, sales rep, or other go-between. That's helpful on many fronts, but it can hinder communication where the menu itself is concerned. If you care enough about the food to be concerned about the details, chances are the chef will enjoy speaking with you and will give you the scoop on what his or her kitchen does best.

* Always explore local, seasonal options first. It's good for your wallet and for the environment.

* Look for leverage points that can help you lower your costs. For example, if you are working with the same vendor for food and drinks, and you know they're making an immense profit on booze, start low when discussing the number of bottles you want to buy. Later, suggest that you might actually want to buy twenty bottles of champagne instead of fifteen—but only if they can throw in that extra appetizer you'd been discussing for free.

* Ask at your venue if there's anything at all that they'd allow you to bring in from another source—cake, mints, chocolate fountain, ice cream truck, you name it.

* Know your budget, and stick to it. Don't be wowed by special extras introduced late in the game, and don't get talked into things you don't really want or need. "Keep it simple" is your mantra.

* Be patient. Hold out for a while. If you allow the menu and pricing to come together over a period of weeks, and refrain from appearing to be completely sold on a particular menu, you may find that the options or prices get better as time passes.

* Always be respectful, collaborative, and as charming as you possibly can be. Make people want to help you and cut you a deal.

Tip: If you don't want to go DIY for the whole meal, but you do want a little homemade touch, consider bringing out cookies made from family recipes, or an assortment of local fruit, after the cake is cut. Fresh fruit can double as favors for your guests. See chapter 7 for more edible favor ideas.

At Your Service

The number of serving staff you need varies according to how many guests you're having, what you're serving, and how it's being served. (Obviously.) Unfortunately, staffing is a complicated art and a caterer's expertise can be very helpful in this area.

For instance:

Need fewer servers
Buffet
Beer and wine only
Hors d'oeuvres on stationary tables

Need more servers
Table service
Bar with mixed drinks
Passed hors d'oeuvres

The ratio of two servers per twenty guests is generally adequate. Once you've thought about what the staff needs to do, think through what will happen when. For example, while servers 1, 2, and 3 man the bar and clear empties, can servers 4, 5, and 6 plate and run hors d'oeuvres?

A Piece of Cake?

If you or someone in your family is determined to bake your cake, go for it. But it's best to attempt it only for weddings with fifty or fewer guests. Investigate possibilities beyond your immediate circle, too, since a few inquiries can often net a terrific amateur baker. (I have a friend in Los Angeles whose dad hired his Pilates instructor to make his wedding cake.) For our wedding, my mom's coworker made us the most beautiful, delicious, three-tiered cake with raspberry filling and elegant, detailed buttercream frosting. We had almost two hundred guests at our wedding, and the cake cost a mere $200. If you really do want to bake the cake yourself, you might also consider making a sheet cake, or several smaller cakes, instead of trying to assemble a traditional towerlike wedding cake.

"WE DID" Advice From Real Couples

"Instead of a traditional wedding cake we had six really good cakes from a bakery in our neighborhood. In order to make the cake table look appealing, we made cake plates at different heights and then placed loose flowers on the table. We made the plates by buying pretty glass plates and glass candlesticks and then gluing them together [using] a special clear craft glue that bonds glass. On some we could tell that there was a bit of glue on the underside of the plate, but the cake covered it. Our cakes cost $175 and the cake plates cost about $3 to $10, depending on the price of the plates and candlesticks."

—Susan Rivera, Portland, Oregon, on her DIY alternative
to an expensive wedding cake

FOOD SAFETY

There's one more little thing for DIYers to keep in mind: Happy events are not exempt from the risk of food poisoning. In fact, weddings are a prime culprit. (I've been poisoned at one; maybe you have, too). To avoid disaster, remember the following four basic principles:

- CLEAN: Wash your hands and all surfaces often, and disinfect surfaces that have touched raw meat.

- SEPARATE: Keep raw meat separate from all other foods.

- COOK: Cook meats to the proper temperature.

- CHILL: Refrigerate items promptly and keep them adequately chilled.

- If you have an outdoor buffet, don't let food sit for more than a few minutes in the hot sun, and when in doubt throw it out! See: www.foodsafety.gov, www.fightbac.org, or www.homefoodsafety.org.

DIY Decorations

A DIY cake deserves decorations with a sense of humor:

* Icing letters from a supermarket have a fun, appealing retro look. Use them to brand your cake with your names and the date or a quote.

* In late spring, summer, or early fall, simply cover the cake with luscious piles of fruit, such as berries, lady apples, apricots, or clusters of grapes.

* Real flowers are perfect on a cake anytime. Just make sure they haven't been sprayed with anything nasty and that they're durable.

* Consider serving each slice with a drizzle of complementary sauce, like raspberry, lemon, caramel, or chocolate.

Don't try to write on the cake with icing—it will only end in disappointment. According to bakers in the know, only trained pastry chefs and architects should attempt writing on a special cake.

CAKE ALTERNATIVES

Consider one or several stacks of sweets on pretty cake plates in lieu of a cake: a pile of Hostess Twinkies, a tower of cupcakes from a local bakery, or a mound of profiteroles glazed with caramel, à la the *croquembouche* (literally, "crunch in the mouth"), the traditional French wedding cake. Or assemble a table full of pies—that way there's still something for you and your spouse to cut!

The DIY Bar

You can save tons of money by handling drinks yourself. Even if you use catering services, ask if you can provide your own liquor. (And make sure the store that sells you the liquor will take back unopened bottles, in case you have any left over.) If you're running the show, convince or hire some responsible friends to play bartender. If you'd like to offer guests a full bar, outfit your bartenders with the basics: beer, red and white wine, gin, vodka, rum, and bourbon, plus plenty of mixers. Or narrow the field a bit—most people will happily drink whatever you put in front of them, and a carefully edited drink menu can actually make an event feel more special.

Here are some ideas:

* A crisp pilsner beer, rosé wine, and gin-and-tonics for a summer garden wedding

* Champagne to mix with different fruity liqueurs (Chambord, Pama, crème de cassis) for an early evening cocktail reception

* Hard apple and pear cider for a fall celebration

Always go local—many people love discovering locally produced beers and wines that they'll always associate with your big day. Consider featuring a signature cocktail that reflects the wedding's location or atmosphere. You can adapt an established recipe (see www.epicurious.com or www.webtender.com) or make up an entirely new one. Then give the drink a fun name and make bar signs promoting it. But do make sure any featured drink isn't too labor-intensive—your bartenders will thank you.

If you have fewer than fifty people at your wedding, you can keep things even simpler by setting up a no-host bar. Limit the alcoholic options to beer, wine, and a premixed drink or punch—you don't want people mixing their own drinks. Reduce congestion around the bar by offering a wine table, a beer table, and a punch table. For an outdoor reception, stash cold beers in old washtubs filled with ice or classic rectangular Coleman coolers (which are well-made and affordable and come in several colors and finishes, including stainless steel). Remember to assign someone to periodically open bottles, clear empties, and make more punch.

Tip: If you're making up custom cocktail napkins, why not go beyond your names and the date? Try little-known facts about the two of you as a couple— or each of you as individuals. (Your stats on one color, his on another.) These can be great conversation starters, especially when the two families and sets of friends are mingling for the first time. Try www.foryourparty.com for printing.

BE GREEN

It's hard to avoid disposable dishware when you're entertaining a crowd; it's even harder when you're forgoing professional catering help. Luckily there are options that use highly renewable resources and decompose quickly—try www.greenhome .com for an astounding assortment of disposable plates, cups, and napkins that are minimally harmful to the Earth. They sell everything from compostable cups to sturdy plates made from bagasse (sugarcane stalk) and bleached with hydrogen peroxide (rather than with the nasty chemicals used to bleach other white paper products) to biodegradable, heat-resistant cutlery and biodegradable straws made from corn! Their items are available in large quantities at reasonable prices.

How Much Liquor?

Even if you aren't supplying your own liquor, chances are that you'll still have to estimate how much your guests will drink, and prepurchase that amount. Try to negotiate a full refund for any unopened bottles you return.

Here are some tips to help with your calculations:

* Plan for two drinks per person for the first two hours of the party, and then one drink per person for every hour thereafter. (Remember that this per-person estimate reflects a range of guests' behavior—from teetotalers to heavy drinkers.)

* Consider the time of day, how much and what kind of food you are serving (plan to provide more drinks if the food is salty), and what you know about your friends' and families' drinking habits.

How many drinks does each bottle serve? Use the guide below to assist you in your calculations:

* One bottle of wine = 5 generous glasses; one case (12 bottles) = 60 glasses

* One bottle of champagne = roughly 7 moderate glasses; one case (12 bottles) = 82 glasses (Your champagne obviously will go farther if you are only pouring a small amount for toasts. If you want to stretch your champagne, be sure to ask the servers for light pours.)

* One quart of liquor = 21 drinks, when using a 1.5-oz jigger to pour

* One gallon of punch = approximately 24 servings, if you're using small punch glasses

* One pound of coffee = 60 to 80 cups (Decaf-to-caf ratio depends on time of day. But at most weddings, the majority of guests will drink caffeinated.)

Remember that many guests may abandon their glasses mid-drink and get another—people aren't very waste-conscious when there's an open bar. But you can make your liquor last longer by using the "cater pour" (in other words, a dainty amount) for all liquor, especially wine. (No one should be walking around with a brimming wineglass.) Also, use *little* glasses for everything except beer.

Don't neglect the nonalcoholic options. Offering some alcohol-free choices that are as special and appealing as the alcoholic drinks saves on cash and hangovers.

Tip: The Web site www.evite.com has a handy little drink calculator for parties.

BUBBLY FOR LESS

Do you want to run out of bubbly before the toasting ends? I didn't think so! Here are four delicious sparkling wines for under $15 a bottle:

- Saint Hilaire Limoux Blanc de Blanc Brut, from Languedoc. This one has the distinction of being France's oldest sparkling wine *and* the house "champagne" at Paris Las Vegas. Ooh la la!

- Segura Viudas NV Aria Brut, from Catalonia. Most *cava*, or sparkling white wine from Spain, is easy on the wallet, so taste around and find one you like if this one isn't readily available.

- Zardetto NV Prosecco Brut, from Veneto. Ditto *prosecco*, from Italy—good, reasonably priced options abound.

- Lindauer NV Brut, from New Zealand. This sparkling wine gets excellent marks from bubbly-lovers.

One note of caution: Never buy large quantities of any kind of wine without tasting it first. Also remember that most of us are used to buying wine at retail prices—which are much lower than the inflated prices you'll be quoted if your caterer is providing your liquor. To me, there's nothing more galling than paying high food-service prices for mediocre wine. So, even if your caterer is taking care of the liquor, try your hardest to get an exemption for the wine, or for the bubbly, if nothing else. You'll pay less, and get a higher-quality product. And, if you succeed, try to cut a deal with the liquor store! They'll likely be happy to give you some kind of price break if you're buying a couple of cases or more.

Setting the Table

No matter how big the crowd, there's a certain amount of equipment you'll need.

Here's a comprehensive list of what you may need to procure:

* Bar tools

* Chafing dishes, to keep things warm

* Coffee/tea service (including cups)

* Cutlery

* Dishwashing facilities

* Glasses (wineglasses, all-purpose glasses)

* Plates

* Linens (tablecloths and napkins)

* Pitchers for water and bar items

* Plates

* Rags and towels for cleanup

* Serving utensils (including cake set)

* Trays, for passing hors d'oeuvres and drinks, and clearing away used dishes. One really fun DIY idea: decoupage sentimental photos onto the trays that will be used to serve and clear drinks. (Make sure the trays don't weigh a ton, or your servers will hate you!)

* Urn for hot water

Everything but the Kitchen Sink: Serving Tips

* Good-looking serving dishes go a long way toward setting the mood of a meal. An eclectic collection is fine, and it's fun to

unwind during wedding-planning season by collecting them at flea markets and garage sales.

* There's no such thing as too much ice—get more than you think you need. If you need to put all the drinks on ice, such as at a picnic, you need one pound of ice per person.

* When buying paper cocktail napkins, figure on one per guest for each hour of the party. But, as is the case with ice, there's really no such thing as too many napkins—so get more than you think you need. (Remember www.greenhome.com as a great source for eco-friendly paper options, and make sure to have paper towels or, even better, reusable cloth rags available so folks don't use the expensive napkins to clean up spills.)

* Even at a casual affair, go for fabric tablecloths and dinner napkins—they make everything more festive. Renting linens costs very little, and the rental service will wash 'em for you! Or you can get them at discount or closeout stores or estate sales, and mix and match. For a picnic-style event, bright-colored dish towels make great napkins. For a very small event (twenty-five to fifty people), consider cloth cocktail napkins, too—they're elegant and good for the environment. They could even make great favors, especially if they're embroidered with a fitting icon or your initials and the date of the event. Put up signs at the bar telling guests that the napkins are theirs to keep.

* Simple doesn't mean stingy. Whatever you're serving, make sure there's plenty of it. But also set your guests' expectations about the food in your invitation, specifying dinner, brunch, cocktails and hors d'oeuvres, coffee and dessert, cake and punch—whatever you're serving.

* Local high schools and youth centers can be good resources for finding affordable servers and cleanup help. (In my husband's

Ohio hometown, hiring local kids for extra help is such a common practice that the helpers have a nickname, "Kitchen Libbys," and there's even a club at the high school, like the chess club or pep squad!) Or ask young friends or relatives for names. Hold an informal casting call. If they're responsible enough to show up for the interview, they should make it to the wedding.

* Consider bringing in a local vendor to serve a special treat, like mini doughnuts, frozen confections from an ice-cream truck, empanadas, or tamales. Troll festivals for inspiration. Guests love these quirky, unexpected touches and will remember them forever.

Deep Breath: Eat, Drink, and Be Married

Perhaps the cardinal rule regarding food at a DIY wedding is that it shouldn't stress you out so much that you lose your own appetite. Be as involved or as hands-off as you wish. Enjoy the tastings. Enjoy testing recipes. Enjoy the process. Pour yourself a big glass of wine. And breathe.

FLOWERS

CHAPTER SIX

If flower arranging is your specialty, and/or you're a fairly low-maintenance type, full-on DIY flowers are doable. But because flowers are so delicate and time-sensitive—they need to be handled carefully, and assembled as close to the time of the wedding as possible, for maximum freshness—they may be treacherous territory for most brides. Instead of trying to do them all on your own, why not delegate them to someone in your network, or perhaps do all the planning and purchasing yourself and hand the day-before and day-of work over to a talented friend? Then, on your wedding day, you can say "For me? You shouldn't have!"

Flower Basics

While you're dreaming up options for your wedding flowers, spend as much time as possible at botanical gardens, flower stores, and farmers' markets, asking questions and making notes about what appeals to you. Also, spend some time in the craft section of your bookstore, leafing (ha!) through flower books. You'll likely learn the names of blooms you've admired for years, and you'll become familiar with types you've only heard about. (For a good basic visual primer on flower varieties, visit the flower library at www .aboutflowers.com. And *Martha Stewart Living* magazine's Web site

[www.marthastewart.com/living] has a great "Encyclopedia of Plants" in its gardening section.)

Floral design is deceptively tricky. Anyone who's tried to arrange a bouquet of grocery-store flowers in a vase knows that you need to have a knack for it. I spent a year working weekends in a posh flower store in San Francisco, and I was constantly in awe of the really talented designers.

Here are some basic tips I picked up that will help you create great floral arrangements for any occasion:

* Buy the freshest, highest-quality flowers available. Choose buds that are somewhere between tightly closed and fully open, depending on how soon you want to use them. In a pinch, you can get cut flowers to open faster in warm water or warm air, but never place them in direct sunlight.

* Hydrate blooms immediately upon arriving home. Use a sharp knife to trim a bit off the bottom of each stem, on the diagonal (to expose maximum surface area), and plunge them into cold water. Using a knife ensures a clean cut and minimal damage to the stem.

* If you're arranging in a clear glass vase, the way the stems look underwater matters. (Every stem should go all the way to the bottom of the container, for uniformity.) If you're afraid that the stems might start to look messy, use opaque containers; sometimes the most interesting arrangements begin with a really cool container.

* Before you add the flowers, add a drop or two of bleach to the water in your container to help keep them fresh.

* Select all the stems you want to use for an arrangement before you begin, and lay them out on your work surface or put them in a bucket. Use odd numbers of each flower—three, five, or seven, depending on how big the final arrangement will be—in a mixed bouquet.

* Build the color scheme just as you would when putting an outfit together or decorating a room. The prettiest arrangements are neither monochromatic nor too jumbled up with lots of different hues.

* Don't forget the greenery—sometimes the most striking elements of a floral arrangement aren't flowers at all. You may have interesting choices in your own yard or in a nearby park (just don't get caught!).

* If you're not sure what goes with what, play it safe by selecting a single flower and using them in large quantities. Masses of a single type of flowers like roses, tulips, daffodils, ranunculus, peonies, or daisies look brilliant. But if you have an especially interesting bloom, or a really large or showy flower—a giant dahlia or a water lily, for example—don't be afraid to display it solo in a cool container.

* Your "stems" can include anything you can attach to a floral pick or chopstick: a piece of fruit, a Christmas tree ornament, a bow.

* If you're using a small- to medium-size vase, don't be afraid to cut the flowers far down so the blooms are just peeking over the top of the vase and no stems are visible. Low and tight arrangements look lovely and polished and are usually easier to pull off than taller arrangements. Just make sure that there's a pleasing balance between size of vase and quantity of blooms, since you don't want to end up with too much vase and not enough flowers. Let the size and shape of the container be your guide.

* Using a knife, strip off all leaves below the water level. Take the thorns off roses; strip extra leaves off tulips. The cleaner and smoother your stems, the easier it will be to maneuver them when you start arranging.

* Arrangements should look nice from all angles, but they need to have a focal point. The first flower(s) you put in are your visual anchors, so start with your biggest blooms and make sure that one of them looks you squarely in the eye.

* Be conservative when cutting the stems. You can always take them down another inch, but you can't add length.

* Ribbon or raffia tied around the container helps the arrangement look finished. Experiment with various colors, textures, and widths.

* Change the water in your arrangement every other day, and keep it out of direct sunlight. Flowers last longer when stored in cool places.

* A penny in a vase acts as a natural fungicide—but it may make your stems stand up very straight, so beware if you want a looser look.

* Add one teaspoon of sugar per cup of H_2O to "feed" your flowers.

Creating a Concept

When thinking about handheld and table arrangements, consider the following ideas:

* Masses of anything look great. In general, use a lot of one particular flower, or only a little. The territory in between can look awkward or unintentional.

* Similarly, think big (large single flowers like sunflowers or dinner-plate dahlias for bridesmaids to carry, or for centerpieces) or tiny (a collection of miniature vases with one small bloom each) for maximum impact.

* To create a cohesive look, choose a small range of flower varieties in a limited color palette and use them everywhere you want something floral, or pick a single color and use as many different

flower varieties as you like. Just avoid anything that will look too jumbled and haphazard. Of course, if the event will take place in several different spaces, don't be afraid to try for a variety of looks throughout. Just make sure that the colors are at least loosely tied together, and that in any one space there's harmony as far as the eye can see.

* Don't forget about branches. Depending on the season, cherry, quince, dogwood, bittersweet, ilex berry, or any other kind of branch in tall vases can make striking, easy-to-assemble arrangements. If you have access to a woodsy area with a lot of little scrubby trees, you can even grab branches from there. If the branch omits a milky sap where you cut it, sear it with a match.

* Potted plants make another great alternative, as centerpieces, or, in tiny versions and interesting containers, for the wedding party to carry. Ferns, orchids, cacti, and succulents all make interesting, lasting choices. Potted centerpieces offer a great opportunity to get really personal: a bride and groom who love to cook could use potted herbs or cherry tomato plants; a couple with Chinese or Vietnamese roots could feature miniature orange or kumquat trees, which represent luck in the year ahead. See Chapter Ten for more nonfloral centerpiece ideas.

* If you're getting married anytime from late fall to early spring, consider forcing bunch-flowering narcissus—such as Paper White or Soleil d'Or—so that it blooms the week of your wedding. These plants make clean, striking accents to any table, though their height probably makes them more appropriate for places where they won't get in the way of conversation. (FYI: They also have a pleasant, but somewhat pungent smell.) No soil is necessary, just water; you anchor the bulbs in their containers with river rocks or pebbles. Use a medium-height cylindrical glass vase so that the

stems have some support, or be prepared to stake them—you want them standing tall and proud. Consult your local garden center for techniques, tips, and guidance on when to plant so they'll bloom on cue. (Or try www.easytogrowbulbs.com for more information.)

* In a pinch, don't be afraid to cut up inexpensive potted plants and use their flowers or greens in other arrangements. For example, depending on the season, potted poinsettias, amaryllis, cyclamen, calla lilies, hyacinths, hydrangeas, gerbera daisies, and more may be begging to be liberated from their foil-wrapped pots and placed in elegant vases.

* Outdoorsy or garden-center-inspired touches can work, too, such as shepherd's crooks with hanging baskets (full of things like impatiens, begonias, geraniums, fuchsia, ivy, or lobelia) flanking the entrance to a building for a summer wedding.

* If you can find a way to work the bridesmaids' bouquets and yours into the decorations, you can save a lot of money on flowers. Consider placing unobtrusive vases on the head table or around the cake table to hold the bouquets while you're eating, in lieu of an arrangement. You also can make your ceremony flowers do double duty by moving them over to the reception, if it's taking place in a different space. (However, it's customary at some churches and temples to leave your ceremony flowers there as a donation to the house of worship; in that case, removing them from the sanctuary would be a faux pas.)

Finding Wedding Flowers

You have several options: growing your own, buying from a wholesale flower market, purchasing online, or buying from a local grower (the best, most environmentally friendly option). You can easily combine flowers from a variety of sources. When buying from a vendor, you'll want to find someone who will sell to you at as close to a wholesale price as possible without requiring an unrealistic minimum order quantity, and without insisting that you have a retailer's badge, tax ID number, or an existing account with their business. Farmers' markets are the best places to scout for local growers. Approach them and ask where their farm is located and if they would consider providing flowers for your wedding.

If you live in a big city, your flower market or flower district will likely be quite easy to find—you may even already know where it is. If you're not sure where to find a flower market or wholesaler near you, the Wholesale Florist and Florist Supplier Association (www .wffsa.org) has a "find a wholesaler" link that allows you to search by state. Or you can ask local florists where they buy their flowers. Typically, these markets open to the public after retailers have done their buying, usually in the early morning hours. Plan a visit well in advance of the wedding, six to nine months ahead of time, to scope out the situation. (Of course, keep in mind that the flowers you're seeing may not necessarily be available come wedding time.) Don't be deterred by "wholesale only" plaques in windows. Just go inside, and inquire sweetly whether they'd sell to someone planning to do her own wedding flowers. If they say yes, ask whether they'd do a special order. Then keep shopping. Compare prices at several vendors to determine a reasonable range. Note which vendors seem to stock which types of flowers and plants, and take down contact information for any you really like. If you're lucky, you'll find someone who's willing to help you out for the right price.

If you're having a friend or family member do your flowers, it's ideal to search for a good source together. If you like flowers, the odyssey can be a lot of fun. As you're looking for the right place to make your purchase, you can discuss what you like and don't like, note what varieties seem to fit with your color scheme and price range, and make a preliminary list of the flowers you might like to use. Be sure to get up close and sniff—fragrance, be it good or bad, is important, and you never want to place heavily fragranced flowers around food.

If you're having a very small and casual affair, you may be able to pick up your flowers at a farmers' market, a grocery store that has a floral department, or even a corner market if you live in a big city such as New York. (Costco also has great, reasonably priced flowers.) However, you may not be able to place an advance order at such retailers (though it never hurts to ask), and may therefore be limited to what they have on hand when you go to make the purchase—so this tactic is best reserved for very low-key weddings.

Buying Flowers Online

If you don't have the time or energy to scout for a wholesaler, and you're pretty confident about what kinds and quantities of flowers you want, ordering online can be a good option. In many cases, you're getting flowers straight from the grower, and that's a beautiful thing—they'll be very fresh. To find a vendor, check "Resources" on page 223 for some options I trust, or do an Internet search using terms like "farm-direct flowers" and "wholesale wedding flowers."

As is the case with all online shopping, this approach can have some drawbacks, so *caveat emptor*:

* It can be tough to know exactly what you're getting. Do your homework—about the flowers, and about the vendor—before placing an order. If possible, do a small test order from the vendor a few weeks or months before the big day to determine quality and customer service.

* It can be tough to gauge how many you need. In general, it's best to order more flowers than you think you'll want—that's how you get a lush look, and that's why flower arrangements in general are so expensive. So don't be afraid to go a little bonkers—your wedding

will look better for it. If you skimp on flowers, your bouquets and arrangements might wind up looking underwhelming. If, despite best efforts during ordering, you find that you don't have enough flowers to achieve the look you want, try local grocery stores with floral departments for affordable supplements.

* It can be tough to gauge when the flowers will open, and thus tough to schedule the appropriate delivery date. If you have access to adequate cold storage, such as a walk-in refrigerator (*not* a freezer!), follow the vendor's recommendations. (A regular fridge is probably too small, because most flowers need to be hydrated in big buckets and thus will need to stand upright. But if you can empty it out, shelves and all, you may be able to swing it.) If you will be hydrating them in buckets in a nonrefrigerated space, you may want to schedule the delivery for later than the vendor recommends. Also, take the season into consideration—the warmer it is in their environment, the faster flowers open, and you don't want them to peak too soon.

* Make sure to find out when you'll get access to the wedding and reception site(s) for setup. If yours is the first or only event of the day, perhaps you can set up arrangements yourself the day before. If not, delegate the job to others who will be available right before the ceremony.

HOW MANY FLOWERS?

With bouquets and table arrangements, flowers are counted by the "stem," which is exactly what it sounds like—you pay for the number of stems in your hand, not the number of blooms. As a general rule, you'll want eighteen to twenty-four stems per table arrangement or bridesmaid's bouquet (unless it's something giant like a sunflower, in which case three to five is probably enough); ten to twelve stems for a small bouquet for a mother of the bride or groom or a flower girl; and twenty stems for a robust bride's bouquet. The precise number is a matter of taste, and grip—you'll want to figure out how many stems you can comfortably fit in your hand. If your wedding dress is heavy, you may want a lighter bouquet.

For boutonnieres and corsages, however, you do count the blooms: each boutonniere is one to three blooms; corsages are three to five; and you'll need one bunch of greens per three or four arrangements.

'Tis the Season

Probably 60 to 70 percent of the flowers out there are available pretty much year-round (though more expensive at some times than others), but there are a few types that capture the essence of a particular season. Here are some that I think are particularly beautiful and well suited for weddings:

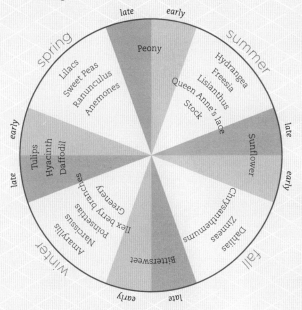

Flowers that are usually available year-round include the following: calla lilies (including miniature callas), orchids (all types), roses (though you will pay dearly for them in early to mid-February, when demand is extra high), lily of the valley (often quite expensive), heather (gorgeous and subtle), and lilies (casablanca, stargazer, and others).

Remember, flowers are brought to a wedding near you courtesy of Mother Nature, who has her own way of doing things. It's possible that a type of flower you have your heart set on may be unavailable (or prohibitively expensive) due to weather or other growing problems.

Hand Flowers

"Hand flowers" is the wedding-industry term for anything floral that will be carried or worn on a wedding day, as opposed to things used to decorate a space. There are five basic bouquet shapes, any of which you can create yourself:

* **Nosegay/clutch:** Bouquet looks like it was plucked from a vase.

* **Cascade:** Flowers fall forward in a waterfall effect.

* **Arm:** Flowers are held in the crook of the arm like a baby. (Hello, Miss America!)

* **Pomander:** Blooms cover a 3-D ball-shaped creation carried by a loop of ribbon.

* **Free form or asymmetrical:** Flowers arranged as you wish— whatever floats your boat.

Tip: When you and the 'maids get those bouquets in hand, your mantra is "Hold it low." A bouquet should be held just below your waistline. Reminding everyone to keep their flowers down is typically the wedding planner's big job. At a DIY wedding, you'll just have to remind each other.

This bouquet has a lush, loose, casual feel. You make it by holding a stem in one hand and adding other stems around it in a spiral fashion. Because it's not tightly wrapped in ribbon, it can easily be stored in a glass of water until showtime. (Do make sure it's dry before it gets anywhere near your dress!)

MATERIALS:

• 15 to 20 stems of fairly long-stemmed flowers (no more than 3 or 4 varieties for a mixed bouquet; if using a variety of colors make sure they are evenly distributed) • Florist's knife • 5 to 10 stems of greenery • 26-gauge florist's wire or ordinary twine • Floral shears • Ribbon for finishing

1. Cut each of the stems on the diagonal and place in water while you work. Remove any thorns by gently scraping them off with a florist's knife (take care not to gouge too deeply) and any foliage from the bottom half of the stem.

2. Take the largest flower in the bunch—this will form the center of the bouquet. Hold its stem in your left hand, between your thumb and first finger, about 6 to 8 inches from the base of the flower head.

3. With your right hand, add 4 to 6 clusters of greenery evenly around the center flower, tucking them in just below the head, allowing the stems to cross at the bottom and turning the bouquet clockwise as you work.

4. Tuck the end of a long piece of wire or twine in between two of the stems, and then wind it around the whole bunch of stems a couple of times to begin to hold everything together. Do not cut the wire.

5. Holding the bouquet in your left hand as in step 2, place 5 or 6 more flowers around the greenery, turning the bouquet clockwise as you work. Secure this next layer of stems with a couple of twists of wire in the same place as before. Continue adding greenery, flowers, or whatever you like to add mass to the bouquet until it reaches the desired size and shape. (Look at it from all angles to make sure you like the silhouette.)

6. Finish with a ring of greenery to give it a nice decorative cuff (optional).

7. Secure all the stems together one last time by winding the wire gently but firmly around several times, and then cut it off and tuck it in.

8. Using floral shears, cut the stems to the desired length, all at the same level. (Don't chop them too short or your bouquet will look top heavy.)

9. Wrap ribbon around the stems to cover the wire, and tie in a droopy bow. If your ribbon is narrow, wrap it around several times before tying a bow to ensure that you've covered all your work. Leave the ends of the bow long and trim them at an angle.

HOW TO MAKE A NOSEGAY

A nosegay is a perfect solution when you want a dense bouquet. This technique works especially well with roses and calla lilies.

MATERIALS:

• 10 to 24 stems of a single flower (fewer for a bridesmaid's bouquet, more for yours) • Florist's knife • Drinking glass or other narrow container that can fit all your stems • Stem-wrap tape • Ribbon or raffia to wrap your stems, or 4-inch-wide ribbon and pearl-headed pins

1. Cut all your stems to the same length—at least 2 to 3 inches taller than you want the finished bouquet to be—using the florist's knife.

2. Get the stems into a compact bundle by plunging them into a tall drinking glass filled with water. You want to get the stems close enough to each other that you can easily gather them up with stem-wrap tape.

3. Come at the collected stems with the tape (still on its spool) and begin taping them together anywhere above the water line, stretching the tape out as you go and winding it around and around until the stems are snug. Make sure that the blooms are aligning into a pleasant shape as the stems come together.

4. Once all the stems are secure, cover the stem-wrap tape with a length of ribbon, winding it around the stems many times in order to cover all the tape, and tie it in a knot. Or, for an even more tailored look, take a piece of fabric or wide ribbon and wrap it around the stems once, folding it over to get a crisp finished edge, and securing it all together with a vertical row of pearl-headed pins. The pins are pushed in at a diagonal so they don't pop through the other side of the stems and poke the person holding

the bouquet. You also could finish the bouquet with real buttons—
either one big one or a series of smaller ones, hot glued or sewn
on, or fastened with pearl-headed pins stuck through the holes.

Corsages and Boutonnieres

A boutonniere is a very easy thing to make, and a corsage is
effectively three boutonnieres lashed together. If you need to make
a lot of them, however, this work can get fiddly and tedious, so enlist
help. Also, consider making a small bouquet for moms and grandmas
instead of the usual corsage. Store corsages and boutonnieres in
plastic bags in the refrigerator, away from anything too cold—you
don't want to freeze them. You can make them the evening before
the wedding, but no earlier than that.

How to Make a Corsage

For a corsage, you'll employ techniques similar to those used to
make a boutonniere (facing page). If you have a really big bloom, like
an orchid, you may only want one flower in your corsage, in which
case all you have to do is follow the steps for making a boutonniere,
adding ribbon to finish, if desired.

If you are using smaller flowers, prepare an odd number (either
three or five) of blooms as described above, and then lash them
together with stem-wrap tape in whatever fashion you desire,
tucking in greens or other small flowers as you wish. (Start with the
flower, and then add filler, followed by greens.) If you don't want the
stems to show, lash the flowers together with their stems pointing
toward each other and their blooms pointing away, sliding the
blooms as close as possible together and covering any exposed stem
with a bow.

If corsages aren't your wedding party's style, try little bouquets for
everyone, or a single flower in each person's hair.

HOW TO MAKE A BOUTONNIERE

MATERIALS:

• Fresh rosebud or other small, hardy flower such as a ranunculus or daisy
• Florist's knife • 26-gauge floral wire • Green stem-wrap tape
• Small amount of greenery and/or baby's breath (optional)
• Clippers • Pencil • Ribbon, if desired
• Corsage pin (a large pearl-headed straight pin)

1. Cut flower stem to 3 inches long, on the diagonal, using the florist's knife.

2. Take a length of florist's wire and gently pierce the green base of the flower, and then push it all the way through. (Make sure you push through a meaty part, but make it closer to the stem than to the flower.)

3. Bend the wire into a hairpin shape.

4. Wrap stem and wire in stem-wrap tape (which will adhere to itself), from top to bottom, in a spiral.

5. If you want to add greenery or baby's breath, line up a sprig with the stem and tape them together with a few more loops of stem-wrap tape.

6. Cut the "stem," including the wire (which may extend below the stem itself), to the desired length using clippers.

7. Wrap the end of the wire around a pencil to form the traditional "pigtail" or J-shaped curlicue that gives a boutonniere a finished look. You can cover the stem with ribbon, if you like, or finish with a bow, but it's probably best to keep the stem small and unobtrusive.

8. Pin on a lapel using the corsage pin.

Centerpieces

When it comes to creating centerpieces and other arrangements for dinner tables, cocktail tables, the cake table, and so on, there are a million intriguing options. Consider placing small potted plants on cake stands, using pitchers or antique patent medicine bottles in lieu of vases, or arranging flowers in a conglomeration of tea, biscuit, or coffee tins (lined with plastic bags to prevent leakage). Anything that can hold water can serve as a container; don't be shy about pilfering from friends and relatives, especially if someone you know is a collector. Again, either go full-on matching or very eclectic, featuring either one striking bloom or masses and masses of the same flower grouped together.

Here are a few additional tips for creating centerpieces:

* If you use opaque vases or containers, then the stems won't be visible, and your arranging doesn't have to be as precise.

* You can line clear glass containers with big, shiny leaves for a sleek look that also conceals stems.

* Another option is to wrap a bouquet of a single type of flower, such as a calla lily, in florist's tape and then ribbon (à la the nosegay, page 141) and then prop it up in a slender clear glass vase filled with a couple inches of water, so the flowers jut out at an angle. (Make sure the ribbon wrap doesn't get wet.) You could even put several bouquets of different types of flowers at different heights in a low glass vase, anchoring them with glass marbles or river rocks.

* If the arrangement will go on a table where people are seated, remember to keep it either very low or so high that it's above the sightline. Anything at eye level will hinder conversation.

* Avoid placing fragrant flowers near food.

* Invite your guests to take the arrangements home with them after the wedding.

HOW TO MAKE AN EASY ROSE CENTERPIECE

I first spied this arrangement of white roses at the Burberry flagship store on Bond Street in London. If you use buds that are just loosening up and pack them fairly tightly, it will look nice and lush and dense when they open. (Put them in a warm place if you want them to open faster.) Go for a monochromatic look, or choose two colors for a checkerboard effect. You could also use this technique to arrange any round, full, straight-stemmed flowers that can snuggle up against one another, such as peonies. (It's harder to do with a sparser flower, such as a gerbera daisy, because the petals will get in each other's way and the blooms won't entirely hide the tape.) Measure your vase and sketch your checkerboard on a piece of paper before you buy your flowers, so you know how many stems you'll need.

MATERIALS:

• Low square or rectangular clear glass vase • Skinny green florist's tape (*not* stem-wrap tape, but the nonstretchy, dark green stuff)
• Enough roses to fill each square of your checkerboard • Florist's knife

1.   Take a low square or rectangular vase and block out an even grid on top using skinny green florist's tape. Take care that the tape stops at the lip of the vase and doesn't come down the side.

2.   Place one rose inside each square of the grid, cutting the stems with a florist's knife so that each flower is just tall enough to stand upright, with its blossom resting on the top of the grid.

HOW TO MAKE AN EASY ORCHID CENTERPIECE

I've included this project to show how a few simple moves can turn a run-of-the-mill plant from a grocery store or garden center into something stunning. For all potted plants, great containers up the ante, dusting and polishing the leaves makes a huge difference, and a handful of moss on top of the potting soil can hide a multitude of sins. But orchids in particular do very well with this treatment—they're exquisite already, so when you dress them up a little they look absolutely dazzling.

MATERIALS:

• Potted single-stalk orchid, such as a phalenopsis or lady slipper,
in a plastic pot • Decorative pot, such as terra-cotta or ceramic,
large enough to accommodate the orchid in its plastic pot
• Sturdy clippers • Natural-colored bamboo stake • Raffia or ribbon
• Dried moss (such as sheet moss, mood moss, or Spanish moss;
buy online at a store like www.driedflowersrus.com)
• Leaf spray • Soft cloth

1. Before you begin, soak the orchid's soil with water and let it drain.

2. Leave the orchid in its plastic pot but remove the stake it came
    with, carefully undoing the twist ties that attach it to the stalk.

3. Plop the potted orchid inside the decorative outer pot.

4. Using the clippers, cut the bamboo stake to the appropriate
    length—it needs to reach just to where the stalk begins to curve,
    but remember to add 2 or so inches for the part that will be
    submerged in the pot.

5. Press the stake securely into the potting mixture, right next to
    (and parallel to) the stalk.

6. At one, two, or three spots, depending on how tall the stalk is and the look you're trying to achieve, tie the stalk and stake together tightly with a length of raffia or ribbon. (The stake supports the stalk, so they should be flush.) Finish in a small bow or square knot with the ends cut off, for a clean look. You also can use the positioning of the stake to gently guide the orchid's stalk in the direction you want to go, if you'd like it to lean more to one side or the other, or stand up straighter. (An angle can look quite interesting.)

7. Spread the moss all over the top of the pot, covering every trace of root and potting material. (If you're using mood moss, break it into large chunks and fit it together like puzzle pieces.)

8. Shine up the leaves with the leaf spray, buffing carefully with a soft cloth. Complete this step in a well-ventilated area, and make sure to wash your hands and the cloth afterward.

Tip: For a larger centerpiece, you could place three smaller orchids, such as lady slippers, in one decorative pot, with each orchid facing out. You could also stake each stalk of multiple-stalk orchids, as long as each stalk has enough space that's free of blooms.

Deep Breath: Nature's Way

Flowers are wondrous, fragile, living things. If they don't turn out exactly like you thought they would, consider whether perhaps they're just being the way they gotta be. Maybe they'll give you some insight into your husband-to-be. Or your future mother-in-law. Or your own mom. Chew on that one for a while. And breathe.

FAVORS

CHAPTER SEVEN

Let me make a confession about favors. When planning my own wedding, I had great intentions going in, and lots of ideas. But somehow I got caught up in the wedding whirlwind, and when the day arrived I found myself without a single gift (besides the dinner, the drinks, the dancing, the hotel goody bags, and the memories, of course) to give my guests. So I thought about everything I *was* giving them, and then I just let it go. And they're all still speaking to me.

Since then, I have a new attitude. Favors are not to be forced—only do them if you can make them truly meaningful to you and your groom. A great handmade favor that evokes warm feelings about the happy couple (that's you!) and/or your wedding in some way can be the *pièce de résistance* of the DIY wedding. But with so much stuff in our lives already, isn't something edible, functional, or charitable probably the best choice? Everybody loves a treat (especially if it's homemade), regional specialties like wine or fruit abound, and something that can be consumed equals less clutter. Useful household items or things to play with make welcome favors, too, but the key is to make it truly useful or enjoyable. Another good option is something intangible, such as a donation to a charity in your guests' names. No matter how much they love you, most people do not need or want a candleholder, mini wedding bell, back scratcher, or other tchotchke adorned with your names and initials. But you already know that! That's why you're here.

Edible Favors

Everyone loves food, whether it's a take-home delicacy or as a little something extra to eat at the reception. A late-night sweet treat is always immensely popular, so consider setting up a table full of goodies at the end of the reception instead of offering individual favors at each table. Hardy, bite-size fruit like cherries or grapes, dried fruit, nuts, candy, and cookies made from family recipes (with copies of the recipes on hand for guests to take home, of course) all work well. Pick whatever fits the theme of your wedding. If you don't already have the treats packaged up into single servings, make sure to set out serving utensils, and little paper or waxed-paper bags (or, at the very least, lots of cocktail napkins) so people can take them to-go. (If you're serving cookies, don't even think about skipping the milk.) You can certainly put treats by each guest's plate instead, but then they'll definitely need to be packaged.

In general, items meant to be taken home should be put at each place setting, and items meant to be eaten at the reception or shortly thereafter can go on a table of their own. The exception would be anything bulky—bags of coffee, jars of spices, or bottles of wine or liqueur (after-party!)—that might take up too much space on the guests' tables.

Send your guests off to bed with a homemade, naturally flavored lollipop tied with pretty ribbon and a tag that reads "Sweet Dreams." You can buy molds, bags, and sticks at craft or specialty stores or online. Or skip the molds and pour out a funky, free-form pop.

Try using tea—black, green, or herbal—in place of water for a more sophisticated, complex flavor. (You can experiment with fruit juice, too, but its additional sugar may affect the recipe, so proceed with caution.) Try pairing chamomile tea with lemon flavoring oil, or green tea with a mint extract, or experiment with anything that evokes the place where you're getting married, such as lavender for the Napa Valley, apple brandy for upstate New York, or fiery hot chilies in Santa Fe. Other natural flavoring oils that are easy to find include ginger, peppermint, and cinnamon. Local restaurants that serve fresh regional ingredients in inventive ways can be a font of flavor-combination ideas—study their dessert menus.

The following recipe makes one dozen lollipops. You can double it, but that's the biggest batch you should attempt to make at one go. Have a helper on hand if you're doubling, since you have to work quickly with molten candy. Lollipops can be made up to two weeks ahead if stored in a cool, dry place.

MATERIALS:

• Lollipop molds, if desired • Cooking spray, such as Pam • 12 lollipop sticks • Baking sheet • Aluminum foil • 1 cup sugar
½ cup water (or brewed tea) • 2 tablespoons light corn syrup
• Handheld candy thermometer • Cooling rack • 4 to 8 drops food coloring (or go without, for a pretty caramel color)

• 2 to 3 drops flavoring oil (preferably natural oil from a health-food store, as opposed to synthetic oils) • 12 lollipop bags • Ribbon or raffia to tie • Tags, if desired, with small hole punched to affix to tie

1. Spray molds with cooking spray and set up sticks according to directions on package. It's wise to also coat all surfaces that might encounter the hot sugar—spatulas, etc.—with cooking spray. If you're making free-form pops, line a large baking sheet with aluminum foil; spray lightly with cooking spray; and space lollipop sticks evenly.

2. In a heavy saucepan over medium heat, combine sugar, water or tea, and corn syrup, then heat, stirring, until sugar dissolves. Cover and boil mixture 1 minute.

3. Remove cover and boil the syrup until it reaches 310°F (154°C), also known as the "hard-crack stage," on your candy thermometer.

4. Immediately remove the saucepan from the heat and set it on a cooling rack. Let the syrup cool for 5 minutes.

5. Stir in your food coloring and flavoring. If you are making multiple batches, make a note of how many drops of each you use so that the color and flavor are consistent among batches.

6. Quickly pour syrup into molds, or into 2- to 3-inch-wide puddles at one end of each stick. Allow candy to cool completely before removing the pops from the molds or baking sheet, placing them in bags, tying them with ribbon, and adding tags.

Mix-and-Match Treats

Little parcels of goodies will make all your guests smile—and you don't have to wrap a single thing in tulle. Also, if you have a beautiful little container, don't feel compelled to stuff it full. Sometimes a single object—a beautiful candy egg for a springtime wedding, or a solitary petit four for an afternoon event—can be even more striking than loads of stuff.

To get your wheels turning, check out the following list of ideas. Pick a container from column A and filler from column B. And if it's an open container, tuck in a little name card and—voilà—place cards.

CONTAINERS

* Pure white muffin cups (double- or triple-layered for heft)
* Handmade origami boxes
* Small clear or colored plastic boxes
* Chinese takeout containers (faux from a paper store or real from a restaurant)
* Sake cups or handle-less teacups
* Tiny paper sacks
* New York City coffee cups (bought by the sleeve from a coffee-cart guy)
* Kitschy shot glasses
* Delicate soap dishes
* Vintage pillboxes
* Eyeglass cases
* Mini martini shakers
* Linen sachets

FILLERS

* Salted mixed nuts
* Jordan almonds
* Nonpareils
* Fresh cherries
* Hershey's kisses
* Dried fruit
* Custom M&M's
* Custom fortune cookies
* Conversation hearts
* Red hots
* Gumballs
* Popped popcorn
* Gummi anything
* Saltwater taffy
* Margarita-flavored jelly beans
* Peppermints
* Chocolate-covered pretzels

HOW TO FOLD AN (OPEN-TOPPED) ORIGAMI BOX

Origami is an elegant, precise Japanese art form that uses no paper or glue. Unfortunately, it can be extremely frustrating to try to learn this art from a book—the best way to master it is by watching someone else fold. Hence, I gratefully refer you to the glorious Internet: the Web site www.expertvillage.com has an excellent short instructional video. Experiment with different papers until you find one that folds easily enough for your taste but also holds up to whatever you want to put inside of it. All origami begins with square paper, so if your paper of choice doesn't come that way you may want to take it to a copy shop and cut it there (unless you've invested in a small paper cutter). A 6-inch square of paper will net you a square box that's 3 inches wide and 1 inch tall.

Hotel Goody Bag Treats

Any snacks or little gifts you leave for your guests when they check in to a hotel can be considered favors as well—and here's a good opportunity to get the groom's family in on the act. Consider having them contribute treats with regional significance. At our wedding, for example, the chocolate-and-peanut-butter "buckeye" candies celebrating my husband's Ohio heritage were quite a hit. But the single best wedding favor I've ever encountered was the following snack mix. It was all anyone talked about all weekend, besides how beautiful the bride looked. It also goes great with a late-night beer.

HOW TO MAKE JEAN GURUCHARRI'S AND SALLY ABROMOVICH'S CRACKER MIX

INGREDIENTS:

• 1 box triangular Triscuits • 1 box White Cheddar Cheez-Its
• 1 box Wheat Thins • 1 box cheese mini Ritz sandwich crackers
• 1 box crackers of your choice—double up on one of the above or pick something new • Large roasting pan • 1 cup vegetable oil
• 2 packages dry Hidden Valley Ranch dressing • ⅛ to ¼ teaspoon cayenne pepper • 1 teaspoon dill weed • Small waxed paper or cellophane bags • Ribbon, if desired

1. Preheat oven to 225°F.

2. Mix all crackers together in a large roasting pan.

3. Combine oil, dry ranch dressing mix, cayenne pepper, and dill weed in a bowl; pour over crackers and mix well to coat.

4. Bake in oven, uncovered, for 2 hours, stirring every 30 minutes.

5. Turn oven off and leave pan in oven overnight to cool.

6. When completely cool, package into the small bags and tie with the ribbon.

Each batch should yield enough mix for eight generous helpings. You can easily double the recipe and make two batches at once—just make sure you have two roasting pans. And you can keep the mix in the fridge for up to one month. It also freezes well, so you can work ahead and store it in an airtight container in the freezer until you've got enough for all your guests. The day before the wedding (or the day before your guests will be checking into their hotel), package them up and staple shut or tie with ribbon. If you're feeling particularly generous, attach the recipe, too!

Although you shouldn't neglect out-of-towners who might be staying at private homes rather than hotels, you don't have to drive yourself crazy in the days before the wedding running around town dropping off goody bags. Unless guests are staying with a close friend or relative, you can hand out their bags at the rehearsal dinner or morning-after brunch, if you're having such events. But if you don't manage to distribute all of them, don't sweat it—under no circumstances should your goody bags be a significant source of stress. Just do whatever moves you, and call it good.

Tip: A poem or quote that captures the spirit of the place you're getting married makes a goody bag extra special. Peruse works by local authors for just the right reference, then type it up, print it out, and staple it onto the front of each bag so it doesn't get lost or overlooked.

"WE DID" Advice From Real Couples

"For our welcome baskets in the hotel rooms, we found a bakery that would let us develop our own cookies. We found cookie cutters that matched our theme—mountains, evergreen trees—and the bakery used them to make a few samples. We picked the final frosting colors and they made two hundred cookies for us for $1.50 per cookie. We bought the bags wholesale and put in some bottled water from Costco, postcards of Mt. Hood that we bought directly from the photographer for 75 cents each, tissue paper from the dollar store, and a note from Kelly and me that included information on local restaurants. I think it made a nice welcome at very little cost."

—Cindi Chandler Polychronis, on her wedding to husband
Kelly in the forest near Mt. Hood, Oregon

Useful/Dual Purpose Favors

Everyone has a different definition of *useful*, I suppose, but what I'm really talking about here is something that's not purely decorative, whether it's designed for utility or entertainment.

Here are some ideas:

* If the weather is likely to be hot, put a pretty straw fan on each chair before the ceremony. You can put a tag on the handle with your names and the date, if you desire.

* For an intellectual crowd, try bookmarks or bookplates printed with your names and the date, packaged in glassine envelopes for safekeeping.

* For a rowdier crowd, create custom temporary tattoos with your names and the date—there are lots of Web sites that offer this service.

* It's easy to make personalized crossword puzzles and word searches using free or low-cost software found online. (Try www.crosswordweaver.com.) Hand them out with pens or pencils printed with your names and the date.

* An ingredient and matching recipe will extend delicious memories of the weekend into your guests' own homes—think small potted basil plants with instructions for making pesto, or a tiny jar of perfectly proportioned spices with a (formerly) secret family curry recipe.

* Who doesn't love fragrant homemade bath salts? It takes seconds to make them from sea salt, kosher salt, or Epsom salts and essential oils. Choose a scent that evokes the time and place of your wedding, and package them in small screw-top or cork-topped glass jars (www.save-on-crafts.com has a good selection at affordable prices). Recipes abound on the Internet, so choose one and

make a test batch a month or so before the wedding and make sure it turns out—and keeps—well.

* One artistic bride I know made coloring books for the kiddies and the young at heart. She drew pictures telling the story of how she and the groom met, photocopied them, punched holes in them, and bound them together with ribbon. She stashed one in each hotel bag, along with an assortment of crayons.

* A homemade sachet full of lavender will keep the moths away from your guests' sweaters.

* Seed packets are colorful, useful, and good for the planet. The same is true of saplings—you can get them for $3 a pop at www.arborday.org.

* Years ago, monogrammed matchbooks were *de rigueur* at fashionable weddings. Today, there are tons of customizable styles available, ranging from kitschy to posh—and all of them make a stylish, retro keepsake that will remind your guests of your wedding, whether they're lighting up or lighting a fire in the hearth. Try www.foryourparty.com for a great selection.

Another idea that falls under the "useful" heading is making your favors multitask. Create place cards out of beautiful, quirky, or useful objects that people will want to save or reuse:

* Tiny picture frames make excellent homes for place cards. Just print out sheets of names and table numbers and slide them in. You can even place a Polaroid i-Zone camera (www.i-zone.com) on each table, or near the guest book, for people to snap postage-stamp-size pics to slip into the frames over the course of the evening.

* You also can make a place-card holder out of any object that can be discreetly slit with an X-ACTO knife to hold a piece of card stock. Corks from wine or champagne bottles work beautifully (a wine bar near you will undoubtedly be happy to unload their extras).

* Any small fruit, such as lady apples, Seckel pears, or mini gourds, can work beautifully, too—just slit the stem and slide the card firmly into place. (Beware outdoor weddings and wind; some fruit stems may be too delicate to hold cards in even mild gusts.)

* Many varieties of seashells could cradle small rectangular place cards in their bowls—much better than the ready-made seashell place-card holders that will set you back $10 or more apiece.

* A smooth stone looks elegant holding a pretty place card flat on the table (a perfect idea for outdoor events in windy weather—you can even stencil the table number, or the guests' initials, on top).

* For a smaller wedding, if you or someone you love happens to have a large toy collection that's ready for a second life, this could be the perfect opportunity to spread the joy. A tiny figurine or stuffed animal at each place can hold a place card on its lap, or in its hands. A Matchbox car could support a place card on its windshield, or a Slinky could cradle one between its coils.

* For a quick and easy (though more expensive) alternative to a DIY favor that still has a high creativity quotient, consider a souvenir from the city or state where you're having the wedding, such as a kitschy postcard, magnet, shot glass, or keychain.

Tip: Making mix CDs featuring your favorite tunes for all your wedding guests is tempting. But it's pretty time-consuming to burn all those disks, not to mention illegal (making one hundred or more copies of a song definitely strains the limits of "personal use"), so it's probably better to skip the CD favor.

Intangible Gifts

Sometimes the best gift is intangible. A donation to a cause you care about—literacy, clean drinking water in Africa, the homeless, an endangered species, heart disease—declared on a small ribbon-tied scroll or a card at each place setting is an easy, feel-good way to be generous and honor your guests at the same time. (You don't actually make multiple tiny donations in the name of each guest—you just write one check.)

Alternatively, aim for fun. For a destination wedding where all the guests are staying in the same place, consider arranging with the hotel bar to set guests up with an extra drink on you, to be enjoyed at their leisure—just make up a small certificate that the bartenders can collect, and pay your tab at the end of the weekend.

Or postpone the grace note until after the wedding: Make sure that the two of you get your (digital) picture taken with the guests at each table, and then, when you return from your honeymoon, use one of the online photo services to create personalized photo cards that you inscribe with a simple note of thanks for being part of your big day.

"WE DID" Advice From Real Couples

"Instead of doing traditional guest favors, we donated the money we would have spent doing that to the Leukemia & Lymphoma Society on behalf of each guest, in memory of Andy's brother Toby, who died of leukemia when he was thirteen (Andy was ten at the time). We thought it was a good way to honor Toby on a day when we really wished he could have been there with us. Plus, it felt a lot more useful to donate money to a good cause than to spend it on trinkets. We printed our message onto green 8½-by-11-inch paper and then cut each sheet into fours. We rolled each up and sealed it with a monogram sticker, then put a 'favor' at each guest's dinner plate."

—*Mary Morrison, Chicago, on her meaningful wedding favors*

Deep Breath: Do Yourself a Favor

When it comes to favors, you have every right to go extra easy on yourselves. You've already spoiled your guests with a lovely event full of personalized touches, and if they've traveled in from out of town you've likely made them a goody bag for their hotel room as well. They don't need much in the favor department—a token will do. If you're dead set on DIYing it, consider making gifts that are suitable for couples—a bottle of wine, some coffee, bath salts—which would cut the quantity you have to make in half...and leave you more time to breathe.

RINGS

CHAPTER EIGHT

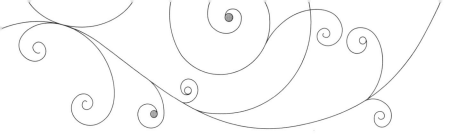

Think about your engagement ring: Maybe you love it; maybe you (secretly, or not so secretly) don't. Maybe you adore it now, but you know it won't fit your life forever. Maybe you don't even wear one. It matters not, really, because, as beautiful as it may be, an engagement ring is technically just a placeholder, a symbol of a temporary state of being. An appetizer, if you will.

Your wedding ring, however, is the main dish. It's a symbol of a permanent bond. It's something you and your husband-to-be choose together, and wear together—until death do you part. When you take the long view, don't you think wedding rings definitely deserve our DIY thought and energy?

Short of taking a metalworking class together—which, when you think about it, would be a very cool thing to do with your time during your engagement—it's pretty hard to actually make your rings yourselves, at least ones as high-quality and durable as wedding rings should be. But there are plenty of other ways to make a conscious purchase—and add a personal touch.

Have Your Rings Made

Nearly every community has a local jeweler or artist who can make you a pair of unique rings. Many jewelers do custom work, even if they don't advertise that fact, and you can find jewelry artisans

by browsing and asking around at craft boutiques and galleries, perusing advertisements in local magazines and newspapers, and calling your local chamber of commerce. Pay attention when you hear enthusiastic endorsements about a particular artist from more than one person. Choose someone who works near enough to where you live that you can meet with them in person as often as necessary to make sure the job is done right.

If you're not sure what you want, shop around for ideas and inspiration before you dive in to the process of custom design. When meeting with potential jewelers, ask to see as many samples of their work as they're willing to show. Don't put down a deposit until you've decided what you want and have had a clear, detailed conversation about your desires.

If you have existing stones or metal you'd like to use, you may be able to cut your costs considerably and be kinder to the Earth to boot (more on that in a moment). Ask potential jewelers whether they're willing to melt down Grandpa's 18-karat gold cuff links, or place a family emerald in a modern setting.

And by no means do your rings need to match—this is one area where no one should have to compromise. Choosing something that reflects who you are as individuals doesn't make you any less married.

Tragic Flaws and Heavy Metals

One excellent reason to blaze your own sparkling path where rings are concerned is that fine jewelry can raise a host of ethical concerns. First, there's the sobering concept of "conflict diamonds": it's a sad fact that profits from the sale of rough diamonds often wind up funding a laundry list of nasty business, from rebel groups in countries like Angola, Sierra Leone, and Liberia to terrorist groups like al-Qaeda.

Growing awareness of this inconvenient, buzz-killing truth has prompted many countries on both ends of the supply chain to make efforts to adhere to "processes," or sets of procedures, that document a diamond's journey from mine to finger. The idea here is to reassure consumers that their stones are "clean." But the efficacy of these processes is spotty, at best, and only limited to diamonds from certain regions. It's a Herculean task to enforce anything on a global scale, so we can guess that some of these processes are unreliable. And, even if that flawless stone isn't tainted by a legacy of blood money, chances are its miners toiled long and hard for very little money in harsh conditions.

Some companies, like Rand diamonds (www.randbrand.com), do offer some peace of mind—but the process is still extremely rough on the environment. Whether diamonds come from deep deposits in the Earth (there are underground diamond mines on every continent except Europe and Antarctica) or are culled from riverbeds, their extraction upsets the ecosystem and harms animals and plants. And because diamonds are a finite resource, mining them is inherently unsustainable. (The same goes for all gemstones, actually.)

The bad news doesn't stop there. Precious metal mining is equally hard on the Earth. Virgin land is continually being destroyed to make roads, house miners, and extract the booty, and the toxic cyanide and mercury used to leach the metals from the surrounding rock contaminates the soil. Prospectors and their nuggets are a thing of the past—gold is now found in quantities so small that conventional, large-scale mining generates at least thirty tons of waste rock in order to create a single gold ring. More responsible, smaller-scale operations don't really help much—even artisanal miners around the world must use harmful chemicals, putting themselves and our planet at risk.

To learn more about gold mining's dark side, visit www.nodirty gold.org. A growing group of jewelry companies, including Zales, Sterling, Kay Jewelers, Helzberg Diamonds, Fortunoff, Cartier, Piaget, Van Cleef & Arpels, and Tiffany & Company have signed a pledge to try to help clean up the mining industry, and source their materials responsibly. But as with conflict diamonds, it's really hard to know what went into your jewelry, and it may be years before anything really gets cleaned up.

Ethical Metalsmiths (www.ethicalmetalsmiths.org) is a trade organization for jewelers dedicated to fighting dirty gold. They will provide you with a list of member jewelers/artisans in your area, • upon request.

I know, I know—what a downer. No one wants to think that something as beautiful and pure-intentioned as a wedding ring might have an ugly past. So what to do? The good news is that as a consumer you have a lot of power: supply follows demand. Make the best choices that you can. To keep your conscience perfectly clear, opt for recycled gold and skip the stones, or choose synthetic gems.

Recycled Gold

Many jewelers create fabulous new designs out of old jewelry, giving it a second life by melting it down and recasting it into new shapes. Ask around for local options, which may include a jeweler who works exclusively in recycled gold, or one who's willing to work specifically with materials you provide. Another great option is www.greenkarat .com, my top retailer pick in this arena. It's an excellent resource for more information on ethical jewelry; they sell great-looking ready-made rings that will help you sleep better at night; and they do beautiful custom work at reasonable prices.

Synthetic Diamonds: The Real Deal

There are ways to create gems in a lab that are chemically identical to natural diamonds—and they look and act the same too. Before you skip to the next section, consider this: would you turn up your nose at cultured pearls? It's the same basic idea. Even jewelers can't distinguish them from natural diamonds without careful scrutiny and special techniques. And no, I'm *not* talking about the cubic zirconia sold on QVC. These are the real deal. If you opt for a ring with synthetic diamonds (also known as "moissanite") or other synthetic gemstones, you could be at the vanguard of a trend that makes the diamond cartel very, very nervous. (Many people will tell you that the diamond market is rigged, and that every single stone is wildly overpriced.)

If you're interested in exploring synthetic diamonds, there are a few good places to start. The Web site www.gemesis.com includes a "where to buy" page with a list of designers who use their diamonds; www.chatham.com includes a long list of retailers; and www.apollo diamond.com has plans to sell direct to consumers (for now, they may sell to you on a case-by-case basis).

Rings with a Past

Choosing rings that had another life before you met them is the easiest way to help protect the Earth and quite likely save money at the same time—while adding a little mystery to your marriage. Plus, since precious metals don't lose their value—and some designs will appreciate with time—buying something made of materials mined years ago is as wise an investment as buying a new ring. Loosely defined, "vintage" or "estate jewelry" means any previously owned piece, but the most sought-after estate jewelry is finely crafted and may be one-of-a-kind. To earn the moniker "antique," a piece must be more than one hundred years old.

Obviously, consider any family heirlooms first. If you don't love a ring as is, you can have it reset, or even entirely remade. And who says your ring has to have started its life in that form? I'm lucky to own a beautiful heirloom diamond ring that was born as one half of a pair of earrings. You can make any combination of stones and metal into something entirely fresh.

When There's History, Get the Whole Story

When purchasing estate jewelry, check for dents, deep scratches, missing stones, and evidence of repairs, such as soldering in unlikely places. Look for metal and maker's marks inside the band. To assist in your examination, bring a magnifying lens or jeweler's loupe, which you can buy online for less than $5. You also may want to tuck a small magnet into your purse so you can test whether a ring is real gold. Place the magnet next to the ring—if the ring moves, it's fake.

If you're serious about buying a gemstone in a situation where you may not be able to secure an appraisal, consider investing in a diamond tester, which will tell you whether the stone is real or not. Some testers can tell the difference between naturally occurring diamonds and synthetic diamonds, but some can't, so if that distinction matters to you, make sure you know the limits of your tester and read the instructions carefully.

Tip: Double check your ring sizes before you start shopping. You can pop into any jewelry store to get sized. Remember that most rings can be resized if necessary, but eternity bands set with stones cannot.

Appraisals

When you're considering a very expensive purchase—and really, that's whatever *you* consider expensive—a reputable vendor will not balk when you mention that you would like to have the piece appraised. Ask for at least a week within which to return the jewelry for a full refund, so you have time to secure an independent appraisal.

To assist with the appraisal, ask the jeweler to put a written description of the piece on the receipt (a good idea even if you aren't getting an appraisal), including materials and approximate age. If a piece contains diamonds or gemstones, ask for an accompanying grading or identification report issued by an independent laboratory, such as the Gemological Institute of America's (GIA) Gem Trade Laboratory. Also ask the jeweler to note on the receipt that the piece is returnable for a full refund if brought back within a certain amount of time.

Find the appraiser yourself; do not take any recommendations from the jeweler, and do not use someone from the store's staff. The best choice is an independent appraiser certified by GIA who does not buy or sell. Ask your friends, or people they know, for reputable jeweler referrals. Jewelry addicts and seasoned collectors usually have long-term, established relationships with certain jewelers who've taken good care of them for years. They can provide invaluable advice on just the right appraiser. (A good jeweler with whom you can consult over the long term is a valuable contact for any jewelry buff. These "consultants" are in business to make a profit, of course, but usually not at your expense. They rely on you to refer your friends to them, and in return they'll give you great advice and reduced rates.)

Estate Sales

Finding a great estate sale is like hitting the jewelry jackpot. In just about any mid- to large-size American city, the local Sunday classifieds (under "auctions" or "estate sales") should have several listings. If you read the listings carefully, you should find an abundance of jewelry items for sale. Jewelry offered at estate sales or auctions typically goes for about 50 percent of retail price, depending on where the auction is being held and how savvy the local shoppers are. The tradeoff, as always, is that finding the good stuff often takes some time: you may find yourself visiting sales over the course of weeks or months, since these auctions are usually conducted in several installments. (But you could get lucky on the first try!)

Before you bid on or buy an estate or auction ring, however, research the piece as thoroughly as you can. Make sure you know what it's made of, and the current market value of those materials; find out who created it and when; look to see what similar items are selling for in other places; and explore any other factors that might make it a solid buy or a silly one. Also, be sure to get the dirt on the auctioneer or the estate representatives. Are they locals? Well-established businesspeople? Check with friends or contacts who are veteran auction goers; they should be able to give you the scoop.

In most cases, should you "win" an item, the sellers will provide a written appraisal and estimate, usually at "retail" prices, so you can see how much money you saved. If you did your homework first, you should be able to trust their appraisal—anyone who wants to maintain their good reputation won't fleece you—though of course you can go get the piece independently appraised as well.

Tip: Check out www.estatesales.net to search for upcoming sales in your area. ⤳

Other Sources of Vintage Jewelry

* If you're shopping in jewelry stores for a vintage or preowned ring, it's wise to scope out as many different options as are available in your community. Get to know the proprietors and their merchandise; ask where they usually acquire it. Shop there on multiple occasions and get a sense of whether the other customers are regulars (a very good sign). Gauge the general vibe of the store.

* Flea markets can be a bit dicey, but if you're confident in your ability to determine what you're looking at, or are more concerned about how something looks than about being duped, have at it. Many small-jewelry-store owners shop flea markets, so you might just be getting an item one step lower on the retail food chain.

* I would exercise extreme caution when buying used jewelry online. If the business has a physical store that you've been to yourself or that's been recommended by someone you really trust, it's probably a safe bet, but otherwise you should steer clear, for obvious reasons: you can't physically inspect the merch, much less get it independently appraised. I would personally recommend

Doyle & Doyle (www.doyledoyle.com), however, based in New York, they operate a wonderful estate jewelry store that has an exceptional Web site. I'd send a friend there to make a purchase any day.

* Don't be afraid of pawnshops—they can yield unbelievable treasures, and the better ones are run by real experts.

* Remember that paying cash can help bring prices down, if you're interested in haggling. However, if you make the purchase on your credit card, you may be entitled to additional protection in case of fraud.

* Again, consider investing in a diamond-testing machine if you're dedicated to DIY treasure-hunting.

Decoding Your Ring

Most rings will be stamped with at least one mark inside the band—the precious-metal content of the ring—but a piece may also carry a maker's or manufacturer's hallmark, and a mark specifying its country of origin. However, not all jewelry will be stamped, especially handcrafted artisan jewelry. Enlist the help of a trusted jewelry professional if you encounter inconclusive marks or no marks at all.

American-manufactured gold should be marked either "10K," "14K," or "18K." Pure gold is "24K," but it's too soft for everyday wear, so it's usually mixed with other metals into an "alloy." European gold jewelry is marked with numbers that indicate their percentage of gold and correspond to the American equivalents (for example, 750, meaning 75 percent gold = 18k gold).

Contemporary sterling silver is marked "925." Estate jewelry also may be marked with numbers from 750 to 920, or 935 to 980. Antique German and Polish silver used a sixteen-part system to indicate silver purity; look for numbers 12 to 16. An "Alpaca Mexico" mark means the jewelry is slightly less pure than sterling. But take note: an "Alpaca Silver" mark means it's not silver at all—it's an alloy of copper, nickel, zinc, and possibly antimony, tin, lead, or cadmium.

Though platinum has been very fashionable lately, it's somewhat rare to find it on the secondary market. It only truly came into its own as a jewelry metal in the early twentieth century, and it's always pricey, even though the purity varies quite a bit. Jewelry that contains at least 950 parts per thousand of pure platinum may be marked "Plat" or "Pt." Jewelry that contains 850, 900, or 950 parts per thousand of pure platinum may be marked "Plat" or "Pt" only if it's also marked with a number that discloses the amount of pure platinum in the mix, such as "850 Plat" or "850 Pt." Jewelry that contains at least 500 parts per thousand of pure platinum, with platinum group metals making up the rest of the total to reach 950 parts per thousand, may be marked platinum as long as the numbers of each metal are disclosed, such as "500 Pt. 450 Ir."

Hit The Books

Wherever you plan to buy your rings, do as much research as you can before you make a purchase. See "Resources" on page 224 for some titles of great books about jewelry that can help you shop smart. Another way to get some price ideas is to do a weekly search on eBay for a couple of months—it's probably the best guide to what's generally available, and at what cost. (Though, of course, if you plan to actually *buy* something from eBay, take the same precautions you would with anything you can't see or touch before making the financial commitment.)

Deep Breath: All That Glitters

Unless you're already planning to sell it someday, your wedding ring's value is primarily sentimental. So choose something you love and will want to look at every day, no matter what it's made of, and no matter what anyone else might think. (Also a good policy for selecting a spouse, no?) And breathe.

THE CEREMONY

CHAPTER NINE

Your ceremony is a great place to exercise your creativity and personality in an extremely meaningful way—it is, after all, the reason for the entire event. A few key decisions here make a big impact on the tone of the day.

But the ceremony also can be one of the toughest parts of the wedding to put together. If a logical place to get married doesn't spring to mind soon after getting engaged—or if the two of you don't have identical visions—it may take you a long time to figure it out. Interfaith couples, or couples who desire a secular ceremony, often spend a lot of time deciding where and how to hold their nuptials. And if you don't wind up choosing a house of worship with an officiant already attached (or vice versa), you'll have to secure the officiant and the ceremony site separately.

My own wedding went down just that way. I was raised Catholic, and my husband is Jewish. Rather than pick one faith over the other, we opted for a civil ceremony in a barn, presided over by a wonderful retired court magistrate who does lots of weddings in the tiny Nebraska town where we got married. (Our florist referred us to her, and that fact offers two good lessons: Word of mouth rarely fails you, and wedding vendors often travel in tight packs!)

But there are many different paths to creating a ceremony that's perfect for you. Remember: wherever you're getting married, all you *really* need is your partner, an officiant, and two witnesses. Or do you? The ultimate DIY touch is in this chapter . . . but I won't give away *all* my secrets, at least not just yet.

Finding an Officiant

Who can officiate at a wedding? The easy answer is . . . there is no easy answer. State laws vary—and change. In various places, a clergyperson, judge, mayor, county commissioner or clerk, state representative, lawyer (Maine), or notary public (Florida, Maine, South Carolina) can officiate. You can get some basic information on the Web—www.usmarriagelaws.com is a good primer—but if you're on the hunt for an officiant, begin your search in earnest by contacting the office that issues marriage licenses in the place where you're planning to marry (probably the county clerk, but it may be a separate local government office, depending on the state). Call up and ask who can legally perform a marriage ceremony, and take down all the options. (If you're not sure what county your venue is located in, go to www.zipinfo.com and hit the "free zip code lookup" button. Select the "county name" box and type in the city and state or zip code.)

Once you know the legal requirements, begin your search. You'll want to start as soon as possible after deciding where the wedding will take place, and keep at it until you find someone who has space on his or her calendar. You don't have to outline the ceremony itself so early, but you really should secure your officiant as soon as possible. So begin by checking your resources: Whom do you know who could oversee your ceremony? Family? Friends? Colleagues? Your parents' colleagues? If you turn up some options you'd be happy with, check their availability right away.

Tip: If a potential officiant would need to travel across state lines to the ceremony, be sure to double check that their credentials are also valid in the state where the ceremony will be held. 〜⊱

Expand the Search

If your inner circle doesn't turn up any contacts, ask your venue's on-site wedding planner for recommendations, or inquire with whomever you spoke to when you secured the space. After that, if you're still officiant-less, branch out to other people you've encountered in the wedding-planning process.

Should word of mouth fail to net you any promising referrals, start exploring civil-service options in county and state government on your own. Go back to the marriage-license office and ask if they can refer you to people who typically perform weddings. If they're unhelpful, dig deeper on your own. Call the individual offices of anyone who holds a suitable post. (To find a judge, go to your state government's Web site and locate the phone number for the court administrator's office.) You may need to make several calls before you find someone who can help you out.

You may want to consider secular organizations that are set up much like churches—with leaders who are recognized as clergy and can legally perform weddings—or a church that doesn't feel like a church at all. Here's a list of some such organizations:

Ethical Culture

www.aeu.org

Ethical Culture is a movement inspired by the ideal that the supreme aim of life is to create a more humane society. (Fun fact: Albert Einstein was a fan.) Its followers believe that ethical principles reign supreme, and they stand for separation of church and state, among other things. The movement has chapters, generally referred to as "Ethical Societies," in fifteen states and the District of Columbia.

Secular Humanism

www.secularhumanism.org

Secular Humanism is a philosophy that "upholds reason, ethics, and justice and specifically rejects rituals and ceremonies as a means to affirm a life stance." Somewhat paradoxically, however, they do perform weddings!

Unitarian Universalism

www.uua.org

Unitarian Universalism is a theologically liberal, inclusive religion offering members a "free and responsible search for truth and meaning." There are more than one thousand congregations nationwide, and you can find one via their Web site.

Breaking the Ice

When you get someone on the line who might officiate, gauge your chemistry. Do you feel comfortable with the things he or she is saying? Do you have pretty similar ideas about the institution of marriage, why one might want to participate in it, and the rights and responsibilities it entails? Also ask:

* "Do you have a standard ceremony that you traditionally use?"

* "Are you willing to let us customize it?"

* "Are you available on the date and time we want to get married?"

* "Are you willing to come to our venue?"

* "Are you available for a rehearsal the day prior?" (If you're planning a rehearsal.)

* "Can you meet prior to the ceremony to discuss its content?"

* "Is there a fee or suggested donation associated with your services?"

Some civil servants may only be willing or able to marry you in their office, which is a totally viable option, and easy enough to combine with a splashier reception afterward. In some places, like the United Kingdom, small civil ceremonies paired with larger receptions elsewhere are quite common.

You could even have two ceremonies: a legal one in a judge's office the week prior to your big celebration, and then a second ceremony for, well, ceremonial reasons, presided over by anyone you like and with as many guests as you desire. No one even has to know you're already married, unless you want them to.

Tip: Logically, the process of finding a civil officiant is far easier in less-populous areas with less-complicated bureaucracies. If you're getting married in a big city, you may want to pursue the quasi-religious options.

Officiant Etiquette

Ask in advance if there is a fee for performing the ceremony. If you have a civil officiant, the answer will likely be no (you pay the county when you get your marriage license, a separate transaction), which means that a tip is the only payment he or she will receive. Most civil servants aren't allowed to accept money for a wedding ceremony performed during office hours, but you should keep in mind that after hours the rules change. A gift of $100 or more is appropriate.

If you're hiring an officiant, or having a family friend or colleague marry you, it's nice to offer to take your officiant out for lunch or coffee for a "get-to-know-you" session in advance of your wedding day. (You can even do this in the days immediately prior to the wedding, if you're getting married someplace other than where you live. This meeting also gives you an opportunity to go over any questions you might have about the ceremony.) When figuring out how much to pay (or tip) him or her, factor in the number of times you met with this person—including any lead-up meetings, the rehearsal, and the ceremony—as well as his or her travel time and total expenses. Write a nice thank-you note and tuck the payment into the envelope. One of you, or someone in your wedding party, can hand the envelope to your officiant after the ceremony. If your officiant can't—or doesn't want to—accept the payment, he or she will graciously return it.

And, yes, your officiant should be invited to the wedding reception, along with his or her spouse or a guest. A verbal invitation and RSVP is fine, but if you're having a sit-down dinner, don't forget to set extra places.

Make-Your-Own Minister

The Easy Route

The Universal Life Church

www.ulchq.com

It's true: absolutely anyone can become an ordained minister in the Universal Life Church, via a Web site. The church, which is headquartered in Modesto, California, has been around since 1959, when it was founded as the ultimate declaration of religious freedom. It's so free, in fact, that the church has just one tenet: "Do only that which is right."

Highly subjective, yes—but also highly effective, if you want a friend, sibling, or other family member to be the one leading the charge on your wedding day. All anyone has to do is join the ranks of what the organization claims is a 22-million-member ministry worldwide—which includes or has included the Beatles (all four of 'em), Johnny Carson, Tony Danza, Courtney Love, John Waters, and yours truly. (The process took seconds, and I got my certificate in less than a week. So if you're really in a pinch, look me up!)

Ministers ordained through the ULC can marry people in most U.S. states (Canadian provinces are more leery of ULC ministers), though getting the ordination certificate itself may not be the only step you need to take in order to make things legal—your minister may have to be registered with the county or state, and that takes some time and paperwork. Be sure to ask your county's marriage-license office whether a Universal Life Church minister is acceptable and whether registration is required. The ULC will support you if your state requires extra documentation, but, again, you and your minister will need to allow time for this to happen. Ideally, your officiant will start the ordination and registration process at least two months before the wedding.

Spiritual Humanism

www.spiritualhumanism.org

Another newer, smaller church in the vein of the ULC, Spiritual Humanism, also ordains people online for free. Its tenet: "We can solve the problems of society using a religion based on reason." Its followers also believe that rituals are central to human culture, hence the movement's desire to ordain people so they can get out there and start ritualizin'. (However, their Web site does note that SH ordained ministers are "prohibited from performing ceremonies that involve exorcism, circumcision, and animal sacrifice." Whew.) Again, if you're interested in pursuing this path, ask your county's marriage-license office about eligibility and registration require-ments. The Spiritual Humanism Web site also has a state-by-state list of ordained clergypeople if you'd like to work with someone who's already ordained.

Note: If you live in New York City, you won't be able to use either of these options. Try Rose Ministries (www.openordination.com) instead.

Even Easier

As of press time, in Alaska, Massachusetts, California, and Fairfax County, Virginia, anybody at all can officiate at a civil wedding ceremony. No vestments or online ordination necessary!

There's a little paperwork and a small fee, though, and laws do change, so do your homework before you decide to go this route.

Easiest

And here it comes, kids, the ultimate in DIY weddings: in Pennsylvania (with a Quaker marriage license) and Colorado (with a marriage license issued by the state), you can "solemnize" your own marriage. In other words, you can marry yourselves! You simply sign the marriage license as officiants and return the document to the county recorder. If you want your guests to witness a more traditional wedding, you can ask anyone you wish to serve as "master of ceremonies"—I know one Colorado couple who had the two fathers do the honors. If you're marrying in that state, though, do check with the county where you plan to wed. Most counties are cool with anyone being the master of ceremonies, but some counties interpret the state law to mean that *no one but* the couple can do it.

"WE DID" Advice From Real Couples

"We had a full-on reception after the fact, but our ceremony itself was incredibly simple. We went for a walk together, in our everyday clothes, by a little creek not far from our house. We each said a few words about what the other person, and the relationship, meant to us, and then we recited the vows we had written together. We looked into each other's eyes and simultaneously said, 'I now pronounce us man and wife.' Then we cracked up, and started crying a little bit, too. It was intense and casual at the same time—just how we like it."

—Mitch Hurnstead, Boulder, Colorado, on his marriage to wife Ali

Writing Your Own Ceremony and/or Vows

If you choose an officiant who does weddings regularly, he or she will have a basic ceremony outline, including vows, which you may be able to customize to some degree. If customization is important to you, discuss it with the officiant before you agree to do business together. Keep in mind that the vows portion of the ceremony should be kept to well under a minute—that includes both of you—total.

If you're starting from scratch, begin by learning what must be said out loud in order to make the ceremony official. These requirements vary from state to state, so, again, check with the office that issues marriage licenses.

After that, ponder these questions:

* Outside of our wedding party, who are the people we want to be involved in the ceremony? How many are there? Can we come up with a job for each of them?

* Are there any readings we definitely want to incorporate? What are our favorite works of literature?

* Who are our favorite poets and authors? (Popular choices for weddings include Pablo Neruda, e. e. cummings, Rainer Maria Rilke, Shakespeare, Shelley, and Elizabeth Barrett Browning.)

* Is there a specific song that we'd like someone to sing or play?

* Have we seen anything at other people's weddings that we admired and would like to incorporate?

* Are there any elements of a traditional religious ceremony—in any faith or culture—that we'd like to incorporate?

* Is there anything of special significance to us as a couple—such as a funny story, a poignant moment, or something about how we met—that we'd like to share with our guests during the ceremony?

* Besides our officiant, do we know anyone who officiates at weddings and might have a ceremony outline they could share with us?

When to Begin Work on the Ceremony

I recommend sitting down to plot out your ceremony at least three months before the wedding. Somehow, it's hard to do it before then—it just doesn't feel like the time. But the last thing you want to do is throw it together at the eleventh hour. So set an appointment with each other, carve out the time, and make decisions together. My husband and I cobbled our ceremony together from a few sources: the script our officiant usually uses, a ceremony we received by fax from a judge friend of my husband's parents, a few personal touches, and a couple of Jewish wedding traditions—acknowledging the families' contributions to our lives at the beginning of the ceremony, and breaking a glass, together at the end.

Whose Wedding Is This, Anyway?

If certain people in your lives are voicing strong opinions about what your wedding should be like, and it's upsetting you, you may want to consider working on the ceremony piece in seclusion. The two of you will hammer out what works for you, get it cleared by your officiant, and then show it to others only when it's entirely set. It's a fitting way to enter married life—taking control of the ceremony that joins you together, and keeping outside voices contained.

Involve Your Guests in the Ceremony

The thing that many brides and grooms love most about their weddings is the "this is your life" feeling that comes from having all the people they care about together in one place, mixing and mingling and discovering the joy of each other's acquaintance. That was certainly the high point for me. Especially if you're having a smaller wedding, it's fun to celebrate the community you've brought together by involving them in your ceremony.

Here are a few ideas for how to do so:

* Have your officiant lead a simple call-and-response that affirms the guests' support of your marriage. It could go something like this: "All of you gathered here today are important to *[your names]*. If you are willing to help them uphold the vows they are making here today, answer 'We will.'" A variation on this theme is to have the parents of the bride and groom remain at the front of the room for a few moments after walking down the aisle. The officiant then addresses the members of the family and/or the entire wedding party, asking if they will support the couple in the vows they are making. You might also include some specific acknowledgments of family members and/or friends at this time.

* Write in a "Peace be with you"–style invitation inspired by that portion of a Catholic mass. The officiant calls for all the guests to greet and/or introduce themselves to the people around them. Ideally, you'd do this near the beginning of the ceremony in order to establish a cozy, congenial mood.

* At an evening wedding, hold a candle-lighting ceremony, where every guest gets a candle on arrival at the ceremony space. (Make sure it's outfitted with a paper cuff to prevent drips.) The bride and groom light a unity candle, and then they use that candle to light the candle of the first guest on each side of the aisle in the

front row, who then lights the candle of the person next to him or her, and so on, snaking back to the very back row. Make sure you provide the officiant with detailed instructions regarding your vision of the candle-lighting ceremony, so he or she can lead the crowd in the ritual without any confusion.

* At Quaker weddings, there's no officiant. The bride and groom simply stand up at a meeting when they feel ready and declare their vows to one another, in sight of the congregation. Afterward, members of the congregation are invited to say a few words out loud about or to the couple. This form of group participation is a warm way to include guests in the ceremony, and it can even stand in for toasts at the reception. If you're interested in using this technique, you could include a note about it in the invitation so guests may come prepared with comments, or you could make it entirely spontaneous. Make sure you have plenty of time to accommodate anyone who may wish to speak. (If your ceremony needs to end at a certain time so the space can be set up for the next wedding, this ritual may not be a good choice.)

* What about making a communal bouquet? Have guests take a flower when they enter the ceremony space and come forward to place it in a vase at a specified time in the ceremony. One woman I know skipped attendants and instead had ushers hand each female guest a flower when she entered the church. During the ceremony, the women came forward and handed the flowers to her, and that was her bouquet!

* Here's another idea that springs from Quaker tradition but also echoes the Jewish tradition of signing the *ketubah* (marriage certificate): have all the "witnesses" or guests sign a wedding document, which you can later frame and display on your wall. You can make one yourselves or have one made by a calligrapher. It also makes a cool alternative to a guest book.

Ultra-Personal Vows

There's been a recent trend in which couples make extremely personal wedding vows, such as "I promise to take Barkley out every morning, no matter the weather, so you can stay snug in bed," and "I promise to let you buy the NBA League Pass every year so you can watch your beloved Cleveland Cavaliers play every single game."

They're cute, and they typically get a polite laugh from the crowd, but will they really stand the test of time? As you've probably figured out, I'm all for customization, but I think a wedding should retain at least some element of dignity and solemnity, especially here, in the vows. This part of the ceremony is for promises—things you vow to do, come what may. So take the long view. Think about how you want to be treated in this marriage, and how you want to treat your partner, throughout the decades. These promises should become a part of your day-to-day life and serve as guides to keep you on course in the years to come, when life may not be as simple and sunny as it is today. If you intend to take your marriage seriously, make sure your vows are worthy of that effort. Make sure you cover all the bases that are important to you, which may include trust, honor, care, respect, love, support, honesty, and encouragement.

Naturally, I think my own vows were pretty perfect:

"Jonathan, I take you as my husband. I pledge to live a worthy life, and to share it with you; I promise to honor and care for you, to respect and trust you, to speak the truth to you with love, and to cherish and encourage your own fulfillment through all the changes of our lives."

Ceremony Music

Your music choices have a huge impact on the mood of your wedding. Depending on how you set it up, music can be woven throughout the ceremony, from the minute guests arrive until the moment they leave for the reception (or beyond, if you choose to save money by having the same musicians at the ceremony and the reception).

When you embark on your search for musicians, think about what kind of mood you want to establish: strings are softer; brass will be more triumphant; and less-traditional choices, like a bluegrass band, make a real statement.

Live music may not be as expensive as you think. First consider whether there are any musicians in the family who might be willing to contribute their talents, even if they are too young to drink at the reception! At our wedding, we worked my college-freshman cousin Ryan as hard as we possibly could. Before and after the ceremony, he played trumpet in a brass ensemble led by his trumpet teacher, and during the ceremony he accompanied my cousin Caitlin on guitar while she sang "I Will" by the Beatles. We had hoped to convince another cousin, Sarah, to participate via a pint-size string quartet made up of her fellow Suzuki violin students, but it didn't come together in time.

But you don't have to resort to child labor. If friend and family resources don't turn up any options, consider university or conservatory students. These musicians are often thrilled at the prospect of playing a gig for extra cash; ditto for music teachers at any school, from elementary on up. Ask around for recommendations, put up notices on school breakroom bulletin boards, or call the school's office to ask for names. You may turn up great soloists, or talented people who play in small groups on the side.

If you are hiring live musicians, be prepared for them to ask you what you want them to play. Bounce it right back by asking them what they typically play, and what kinds of music they have on hand (this way you can find out what they're most comfortable with and best at), then branch out from there. If you are using recorded music, you'll of course be making your own choices. So, either way, be prepared to do your homework, thinking far in advance about what kind of songs best fit the mood. Don't be afraid of contemporary songs, as long as they feel right. For more traditional, classical choices, www.TheKnot.com is the best resource I've come across for wedding-song ideas, but it's hard to know how they sound by just looking at a list—and that's the most important part. Thank goodness for iTunes! If you want to scope out a track, go to the iTunes store, search for it, and listen to a snippet. Another great site for clips of baroque music—J.S.Bach and his ilk; great stuff for weddings—is www.baroquecds.com/musamples.html. Remember that you may have to pay for your musicians' sheet music if they don't already own it.

If you're getting married outdoors, it's imperative that you provide shelter for your musicians. If you don't, they'll have to pack up at the first sign of drizzle. (I've seen this happen, and it was very sad. The bride burst into tears as she walked in to the sound of silence. The upside: After a short downpour, the rain stopped, and there was a stunning rainbow.) Also consider whether any of your musicians needs a power source.

THE WEDDING WEBCAST

If you have loved ones who can't travel to see you wed, consider a live Webcast, which, along with up to a month of archived access, will set you back $400 to $750. Check out www.webcastyourwedding.net, www.yourwebcast.com, or www.vowcast.com.

A Civil Ceremony Outline

Here's a list of the basic pieces of a civil wedding ceremony. Just slot in the songs and readings that work best for you, subtract anything you don't like, and you've got a ceremony.

PRELUDE: This pre-wedding music establishes the mood and entertains your guests before you and the wedding party arrive. Begin the music thirty to forty-five minutes before the ceremony is scheduled to start. Choose ten to fifteen songs to cover this time frame, or tell your musicians to play whatever they want, within a specific style or mood.

PROCESSIONAL: The processional is a piece of music that is played while you and your wedding party enter the ceremony space. One song should be long enough to cover everyone who walks down the aisle, but you may want to pick a special tune to herald the entrance of the bride.

WELCOME/CALL TO ORDER: Your officiant says hello to everyone and states what they're there to witness—your wedding. If you want to do a group greeting, or an acknowledgment and invocation of parents, wedding party, or entire crowd, insert it here.

OPENING REMARKS: Here, the officiant should introduce him- or herself and may speak for several minutes on any number of topics: memories of the two of you, if you've had a long acquaintance; a story about how you met each other; or even general thoughts on the nature of love or the institution of marriage.

FREE SPACE! Here's an ideal spot to introduce readings and/or musical performances, if you so desire. Two pieces are probably ideal, be they readings or songs or both. (One would be fine, too, but three would probably be too many.) If you do insert more than one piece here, your officiant may want to weave remarks in between them, and he or she will definitely want to say something reflecting on the material before he or she heads into the next section. Be sure that you give your officiant the readings or song lyrics ahead of time so he or she can write something around them that makes sense.

VOWS: Here's the good stuff, led off by "Will you, Luke, take Laura . . . " You get the picture.

RING EXCHANGE: Each half of the couple, under the officiant's direction, places the ring on his or her beloved's finger and makes some kind of statement. (We used "With this ring, I join my life with yours.") The ring exchange may be followed by other ceremonial rites, such as the lighting of a unity candle, a ritual involving all the guests, or the breaking of a glass. If you decide to have background music during such rites, make sure it's mood-appropriate.

PRONOUNCEMENT: This is the part where the officiant declares the official agency or governing body that has authorized him or her to officiate the ceremony and then says, "I now pronounce you husband and wife." This most likely leads into the . . .

KISS: Self-explanatory.

CLOSING REMARKS: Anything can go here—a blessing or a few remarks by the officiant, or something that you and the groom say yourselves. Or you can even skip it if you want the kiss to be the end of the ceremony. (We kissed and then immediately exited to trumpets blaring "All You Need Is Love.")

RECESSIONAL: Music plays as you exit the ceremony space. Make it triumphant and joyful.

POSTLUDE: If possible, have your musicians go right back to the preceremony music—or perhaps something a little more upbeat but in the same vein—to maintain the mood.

Tip: *Ideally, you'll be the one to assemble your ceremony script, start to finish. Begin with whatever your officiant typically uses, make your modifications, and add musical selections and stage directions for all the major players in brackets. Send your draft to your officiant for review, or show it to him or her several days before the ceremony. When you have a finished product, print out copies for everyone involved in the ceremony and hand them out at the rehearsal.*

Decorate the Ceremony Space

When you're contemplating where to hold the ceremony, remember that you can reduce the money and energy you sink into decorations by getting married and having the reception in the same space, or transferring the decorations from the ceremony space to the reception site (if that's permitted by the ceremony venue). It also helps if the ceremony space is beautiful on its own, with little or no decoration. Finally, remember that when it fills up with people it'll look very different than it does when empty. A touch or two of flowers or greenery—a garland, swags, or wreaths of evergreen or other branches—may be all you need.

Programs

Are programs really necessary? It's nice to show your guests who's who, and what to expect, timewise, but it's also more than acceptable to skip them. (All but one or two copies are going to wind up in the trash, anyway.) I wanted them for our wedding, though, and after much deliberation I landed on a pretty easy—and extremely cheap—way to make elegant, interesting programs. First and foremost, I kept the program language short and sweet so the text of the program could fit on half of an 8½-by-11-inch sheet of paper. I played around until I found a font I liked, and then I had the document copied onto vanilla-colored resume paper and cut. Next, I attached them to a slightly larger sheet of colored paper (I used leaf green, but any contrasting color would do) with an eyelet and spray adhesive (see page 86 for more detailed instructions). As a finishing touch, I used a large rubber stamp of a fern frond, lightly inked with leaf-green ink, to place an image in the center. It looked as if the image was on the paper to begin with, and the whole thing hung together rather well. We got lots of compliments.

You also could take a more creative approach, printing the program on a paper fan for a wedding on a warm afternoon, or on paper cups that can hold iced tea or lemonade. For an outdoor wedding, you could make up yard signs listing who's who. Or you could use a slide projector or opaque projector to display a giant program on a wall, either in a place that guests will see as they enter the ceremony space (in a spot that won't compete with the action at the front of the room) or as something to flash up during the recessional, like movie credits—or even during the action, in opera-style supertitles.

Some brides and grooms choose to introduce the entire wedding party at the beginning of the reception—and that's another fine program stand-in.

Tip: If you do create programs, make sure you get a photograph of one for posterity—they have a way of disappearing! (Do the same with your wedding invitation.)

Deep Breath: You Do

It's amazing how something so simple—he shows up, you show up, some words are spoken—can have such tremendous consequences. Both of you walk away transformed. It's not quite the miracle of life, but it's still pretty awe-inspiring. Step back and savor it. And breathe.

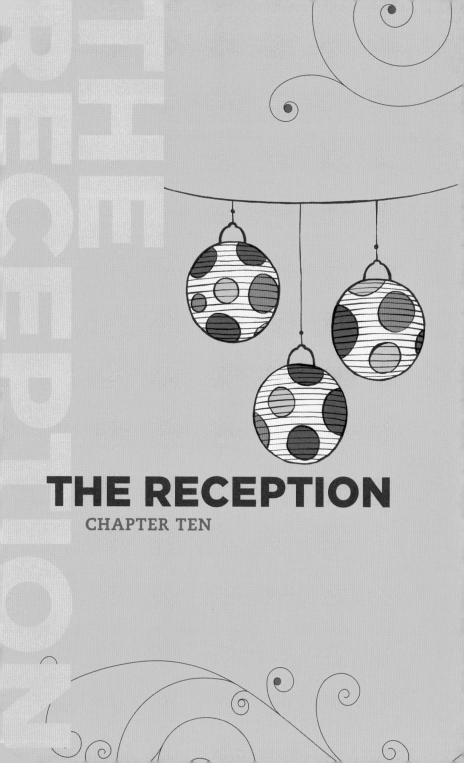

THE RECEPTION
CHAPTER TEN

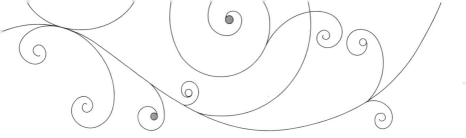

Many of the other chapters in this book offer ideas about planning your reception—how to choose flowers, find great food, treat your guests to fab favors, and so on. So here we'll tackle the remaining reception-related items: decorations and—the most important element of all—music. But first, let's get you there.

There's an art to making the transition from ceremony to reception. Part of the reason my husband and I chose our venue was its potential for a gorgeous, graceful transition: we led our guests from the barn (ceremony) to the lodge (reception) through spring-green woods, all of us basking in the dappled, late-afternoon sunshine. It didn't hurt at all that the path was paved, and that there was a car route, too, for those who couldn't or didn't want to walk. (Remember that you do need to think about accessibility, and the needs of all your guests.)

I think the ideal reception venue has that kind of setup—no requirement that people pack up and drive a long distance after the ceremony, just a subtle change of space, to mark the move from one part of the day to the next. But there are ways to mark it as a transition even if you're staying in exactly the same space. Shifts in lighting and music, and of course the opening of the bar, herald the start of a party.

THE BEST FOR YOUR GUESTS

I think it's safe to say that almost nobody likes a receiving line. Instead, why don't you and the new hubby turn the tables and come to them, greeting people at each pew or row after the ceremony, or asking that people take their seats for the meal, and then going around and visiting each table? Other guest-friendly reception tips:

- Invite all singles to bring a date.

- Allow the wedding party members to sit with their dates.

- Have only a very short break between ceremony and reception, or no break at all.

- Don't even think about having a cash bar.

Decorate the Reception Space

If you're having an evening wedding with an outdoor element, the tools to make your reception magical may be as close at hand as the nearest Home Depot. Japanese lanterns, tiki torches, or Christmas lights all can look magical.

For indoor spaces, one easy, fabulous idea is custom-made vinyl stick-on wall lettering. You can have your names and the date, or a favorite quote, writ large in any font or color you desire. Many different Web-based businesses offer custom services in this area; see "Resources" on page 225 for a partial list.

For a kitschier feel, try a homemade or store-bought banner, or for a flashy approach, consider renting a movable marquee that you can customize with any letters you want—maybe even one with the big flashing arrow on top, pointing to your reception.

Maximize Your Flowers

If you can, make your flowers work double duty by moving them from your ceremony space to your reception space. Proximity helps if you want to transfer any floral arrangements or other decorations from one space to the other. If you must go any distance, it's best not to attempt such a transfer unless you've got access to a spacious van. Be sure to appoint someone to manage the floral transition, and make sure you've got enough hands to carry everything safely. Some good portable floral options include:

- Baskets on shepherd's crooks can easily be pulled up from the ground and carried.

- An arrangement on the altar or on a table at the front of the ceremony space can adorn the guestbook or gift table at the reception.

- Any spray or hanging arrangement tacked to a wall or at the end of a pew could be laid flat on a table as a centerpiece.

Tabletops and Other Accents

Chapter Six has plenty of floral centerpiece ideas, but there are lots of ways to decorate your tables that don't call for a single stem. Consider these possibilities:

* Masses of candles of different heights placed on mirrors to reflect more light and catch drips. Just make sure they're unscented. (Church-supply stores are an absolutely brilliant place to buy simple, unscented candles.)

* Clear glass vases filled with sand, pebbles, rice, or another interesting grain or legume, with candles anchored in them.

* Fantastic tablecloths with very simple centerpieces, such as candles in small votive holders. Colored tablecloths can be cheap to rent, but you might also consider bolts of fabric; brightly patterned oilcloth purchased at a dollar store, five-and-dime, or Latino grocery store; or heavy canvas painters' drop cloths trailing to the ground. Home-supply stores have an astounding variety of drop cloths, and they're quite affordable. You could even choose used ones, for that Jackson Pollock look (perfect for an urban loft wedding).

* Platters or bowls of vegetables or fruit. In summer, try heaps of nectarines on cobalt blue platters; in fall, seductive bunches of Concord grapes or piles of bright green apples in heavy stoneware bowls; in winter, stacks of clementines, lemons, or other citrus fruit on white china. This method is particularly appropriate if anyone in your family collects interesting dishes or serving pieces. If you like, indicate to your guests via a small card on the table that the fruit is part of dessert. (Be sure to wash it before you put it in the bowls!)

* For a fall wedding, a simple scattering of the most breathtaking leaves you can find. Pick them as close to the time of the ceremony as possible, and preserve them between damp—not wet—paper towels, in a cool place, for no more than a few hours. (Do a test run before the ceremony to see how long they stay vibrant.)

* For a wedding at the beach, a pile of sand with a few shells and candles scattered throughout, or sand and shells inside tall hurricane lamps, on each table. Or, for a wedding near a rushing river, you might place a pile of smooth river rocks in the center of each table.

There are plenty of other ways to decorate your space using what you've got on hand. Do you or does anyone in your family collect something that could be of use? Could you borrow a painting, statue, or other work of art that could adorn the gift table? Potted plants that could be placed around the room? A pair of lovebirds in a gorgeous old cage that could sit in the corner? Perhaps something for guests to do outside, such as croquet, *boules,* or bocce, or perhaps shuffleboard? How about kayaking or canoeing, if you're on the water, or bikes for tooling around country roads?

Place Cards and Seating Assignments

First, let me say this: assigned seating is not mandatory. You can save yourself a lot of time and aggravation by skipping the seating chart and place cards altogether. The time, setting, mood, and size of your wedding will help you determine if that's the right route for you. But do know that many people are so used to the drill of "pick up the place card, find your table, sit, make conversation" that a "sit wherever you like" dictum can be a welcome and refreshing change.

For heavy hors d'oeuvres or a light buffet, you may even consider putting out tall cocktail tables with no chairs, and offering a variety of seating options elsewhere. Do consider any elderly or pregnant guests or guests with limited mobility, however, and make sure that they have a comfortable seat from which to watch the festivities. For a larger event (say, more than one hundred people) it is nice to have designated seating, so people have places to put jackets and purses, at the very least.

If you are going to make your own place cards, enlist help. Have the place cards and table markers themselves made up at least two weeks before the wedding—sans names but with a rough idea of who will go where. If you can arrange it so you don't have to make out the actual seating chart and write the names on the place cards until about forty-eight hours before the wedding, that's ideal, because there *will* be some last-minute surprises, in terms of who's coming and who's not (no matter what the response cards did or didn't say).

There's nothing more irritating than finally getting the seating chart perfect—and then having to do it all over again. Make sure you're working off a diagram of the reception space that shows the locations of the entrances and exits, DJ table, dance floor, speakers, bars, and food and cake tables. I divided people up into "pods" of four to six folks who naturally seemed to go together and could be anchored to a particular table, and "floaters" who would need to be slotted into empty spaces.

When you're at about forty-eight hours before the wedding, you can review your final guest list and complete your seating chart. It should be easy to figure out where to seat close family members and the wedding party—knock them out first. Place anyone in a wheelchair at a table near an exit. Put older relatives near enough to the dance floor to enjoy the action but far enough away that the loud music won't bother them.

Tip: It's a good idea to seat younger people who will likely spend a lot of time dancing farther away from the dance floor, which means that the nondancing crowd will have a ringside seat and the whole room will feel cozier and more pulled together. ⌁

My friends Lori and Steve got married in northern Michigan and had their reception at the most darling little inn; it had a big wraparound porch, and shuffleboard on the lawn that gave the band and dance floor some serious competition. Their place cards and table markers were the cutest I've seen. They shrank down vintage postcards using a color copier, wrote a note on the back that read "Thanks for joining us!" and put them in little envelopes with each guest's name on the front. They clipped them to a stand made out of picture-hanging wire with mini clothespins. Each table marker was a full-size souvenir postcard from a travel destination, with a handwritten note on the back about the significance of that particular place to the couple.

"WE DID" Advice From Real Couples

"I just love collecting antique postcards, and thought it helped tell our story since we did a bunch of traveling during our brief courtship. I had bought the cards every time we visited a place, and I frequented used bookstores to fill in the gaps. Also, I love anything with those tiny clothespins—it was the perfect excuse to use them."

—**Lori Kun, on her wedding in Bear Lake, Michigan**

Placecard Possibilities

Here are some other great ideas to create interesting place cards and/or table markers to help guests find their way to their seats:

- To honor a beloved pet, living or deceased, place a photo of the dog with the word "SIT" and a table number in the center of each table.

- Each table could feature a black-and-white photo from a different stage of the bride or groom's life: parents' wedding photo, baby pictures, Bar Mitzvah, First Communion, high school graduation, and so on.

- For the wedding of two bookworms, or a celebration in a scholarly setting, use favorite books—the real things, or copies of their covers—as table markers. Look for editions with pretty covers.

- I made my table markers with rubber stamps, opaque ink, and brown kraft paper. I chose woodsy animal and plant stamps from www.gwenfrostic.com to complement the natural beauty of our venue.

See Chapter Seven for more placecard ideas.

The Guest Book

I've already mentioned various photo-related guest-book ideas (see Chapter Four), and the wedding-contract-as-guest-book option (see page 186), so you can see that I'm all for interesting alternatives. In general, plain guest books that have a line for each guest's name can be deadly boring, and they're nowhere near as evocative as something with photos, or at least with more room to write. Consider ordering a photo album from a Web-based photo service, with a few pictures (of you two, of your families, of one or both of you with special guests) sprinkled throughout. Make sure to leave plenty of empty space, and add a slew of plain, empty pages at the back.

Alternatively, you can purchase a scrapbook and send its pages to your guests ahead of time, asking them to share a few words or images—in lieu of bringing a gift, perhaps. This technique works especially well for showers and bachelorette parties. Shower hostesses can ask guests to bring completed pages to the shower, or the group can take time to create them together. After the wedding, you can assemble the scrapbook, incorporating the predesigned pages, signatures and notes from the reception, and photos.

Reception Music

Great music is the heart of any great party, and that goes tenfold for a wedding reception. Everyone's had the experience of talking to a friend or a coworker who's just been to a wedding, asking them how it was, and hearing them say, "It was OK. Pretty fun, I guess."

That comment—a mediocre review—is every bride and groom's worst nightmare. After years of writing about and attending weddings, I can offer a highly probable diagnosis: Chances are that reception had lackluster music.

There was a time when I thought that the only way to create a kick-ass wedding reception was to hire an expensive, gigantic band.

I've definitely seen plenty of them in action, and I've had an amazing time on the dance floor almost every time. But I've also had my eyes opened to other options—some of the best weddings I've been to have featured a mixture of live and recorded music, or no live music at the reception at all.

If you do have musicians in your circle of friends, definitely consider inviting them to play a set at some point during the evening. (This works best and is least complicated if they can play acoustic.) If you don't know any musicians personally, consider hiring a group that fits the mood of your event—a string quartet, a brass ensemble, bluegrass fiddlers, the mariachi band that plays at your favorite Mexican restaurant, the guys who drum on the subway or in the park. Another great, lower-cost option is to have live music early—during the cocktail hour, for example—and then transition to a DJ or an iPod (more on that later) for dancing. (Or, if you're having a daytime wedding without a dance, keep the acoustic musicians on hand the whole time, for ambience.)

But if you are having a dance, a good DJ—and I emphasize *good*—can make a pleasant party spectacular. A *bad* DJ can hijack your wedding reception, mortify you, and annoy your guests. You want someone with minimum radio personality and maximum flexibility, creativity, and musical knowledge—a wizard behind the wheels who will stay quiet and play the perfect tunes. In short, *you do not want to hire a wedding DJ.* What you want is a DJ who plays at clubs and parties, someone who lives and breathes music but may DJ only as a side gig or hobby. Contrary to popular belief, someone who really, truly loves music will not be snobby and will not subject you to his or her own penchant for Scandinavian electronica (unless you adore Scandinavian electronica, too). Such a person will likely be more open-minded than you might imagine.

To find your dream DJ, start, of course, by asking friends and family members. Also check in with any bars or clubs where you like to hang out. Ask the manager if they ever hire DJs, and whom they'd recommend. Record stores, specifically independently owned shops with large collections of used CDs and vinyl, can be gold mines. Ask the manager if anyone on staff DJs, or if they have any DJs among their regular clients. (Stores like this are often a magnet for people in the community who are serious about music.) You can also check in with local colleges and figure out who the campus DJs are and who's most in demand, although that requires a student contact—anyone in the administration is most likely clueless.

Party DJs may not be as comfortable with the transitions and announcements that are a part of wedding receptions. So if you want him or her to play the role of emcee, discuss that up front, and provide a detailed script, *with precise times and cues.*

We hired our friend Adam to be our DJ, because we trust his taste. But here's the important part: we gave him a pretty specific list of what we wanted. We didn't expect him to emcee the evening—when an announcement needed to be made, one of us got on the mic—but we did expect him to set the mood and keep it going, and he performed brilliantly.

I suggest creating a rough playlist, broken into stages that represent how you'd like the evening to flow, and listing as many songs as possible for each stage. If you've chosen your DJ well, then he or she should own at least some of the music you want. Send him or her your list well in advance of the wedding to see what's available. Be sure to mention that you can provide tracks the DJ doesn't own. Hand over burned discs—clearly labeled—a month or so before your wedding, to ensure that the DJ's equipment can read them. Also deliver any special instructions, and your "do not play" list (a must—and put it in a nice big font). As early as possible, get your DJ talking with whoever is in charge of any audio equipment at your reception venue. Unless you're an expert, that's one relationship that will work better if you step out of the middle.

Tip: Designate someone to make sure that the DJ gets drinks and food. However, if you hire a DJ of a certain type, you may find that the single ladies in the crowd vying for his attention provide him with all the refreshment he can handle. ~§

Questions to Ask a DJ

Don't hire a DJ without having at least one phone conversation. All the while, keep your antennae up and gauge whether you two will get along. Ask the following questions:

- "How would you describe your personal listening preferences?"
- "What kinds of music do you like to play at parties?"
- "What kinds of music do you own? Do you have an inventory list that I can review?"
- "What equipment do you travel with?"
- "If we wind up working together, would it be OK if I gave you some CDs of songs we know we want to hear at our wedding?"
- "How many parties have you played? Where were they, and how many guests attended? Have you done any weddings?"
- "Have you heard any great new music lately that I should check out?"

The iPod as DJ

For a smaller wedding, you can definitely set up an iPod or a computer with iTunes instead of hiring a DJ. Keep in mind, though, that it will be another thing for you to worry about. You'll want to make sure that the sound system is adequate—it'll be a shame if the sound doesn't fill the space. Also, remember that if you're going with anything less than a full-service DJ, you may need to borrow or rent extra equipment to plug into your venue's sound system.

Do your homework first. And keep these general hints in mind:

* Appoint a "music director" who will monitor the iPod all night, troubleshoot any technical issues, and change tracks if something goes awry or doesn't quite fit the mood. This person can also keep guests from commandeering the iPod and picking their own tunes, or even docking their own iPods—unless you want that kind of audience participation.

* As an alternative, ask multiple friends to each provide an hour's worth of music on their own iPods. You could assign each a different mood or stage of the evening.

* Set up and test all the equipment well in advance of the reception.

* Put more music on the playlist than you think you'll need—at least an extra hour's worth. You may wind up skipping some songs along the way, and you want plenty of tunes at the end to back fill.

* Have a backup iPod loaded with the exact same playlist, just in case.

* Make sure that the iPod or computer that's playing the list is connected to a power source and not running on batteries alone.

* Make sure that all the songs on your playlist are high-quality. Listen to each of them all the way through to ensure there are no skips or static, especially if you've burned something off a CD. You may need to spring for new downloads of problematic tracks.

* If you plan to arrange your playlist in stages, think carefully about how long each stage should last, coordinating with the caterer or anyone else who's involved in the timing of the evening to get the best estimates.

Creating Your Playlist

Here are the three most crucial elements of a great wedding playlist:

❶ Variety, in both style and vintage. You want intergenerational appeal.

❷ Danceability. Even the slower songs should make you feel like grooving.

❸ Feel-good quotient. The songs should conjure a variety of moods related to love, lust, and romance. You're creating a little world for a night, so make it as intoxicating as you dare.

When you create your playlist, keep in mind the following:

⁕ Put your artist and song no-nos at the top of the page, in large, boldface type.

⁕ Break your list into stages, and give your DJ an idea of the mood you're trying to foster during each.

⁕ Within each stage, list songs and artists you like and that you think fit the mood. Also highlight any specific tracks you dislike by an artist you generally enjoy.

⁕ Give a healthy sampling of the artists and the songs you envision for each stage, but don't worry about putting the list in song-by-song order—that's the DJ's job. Make sure that you specify "in no particular order," because you don't want your DJ to feel micro-managed—there's a fine line between helpful and overbearing.

⁕ Pulling out a much-loved-but-near-forgotten eighties song is never a bad idea.

⁕ If you do a first dance, dances with parents, or similar, just insert them wherever you like. Make sure that you discuss specific tracks for those dances with your DJ well in advance.

⁕ Be specific about the last song. Make it something that really signals to people that it's time to go, and that leaves them feeling satisfied.

A SAMPLE RECEPTION PLAYLIST

Your DJ playlist might look something like this—plus whatever specific songs you really want to hear:

DO NOT PLAY: B-52's, They Might Be Giants, "Chicken Dance," "Hokey Pokey," "Rapper's Delight"

STAGE ONE: MINGLING/DRINKING (6:00 P.M.–6:30 P.M.)
Nothing so raucous that it gets in the way of conversation, but do play stuff that will begin to help the crowd get loose.

STAGE TWO: EATING/MINGLING, EARLY "HAPPY FEET"
(6:30 P.M.–7:45 P.M.)
Please announce that the buffet is open at the beginning of this stage. Guests should find themselves tapping a toe and, from time to time, exclaiming "I love this song!" If people are looking around wondering if it's OK to begin the dancing, this stage is a success.

OUR FIRST DANCE: BOBBY DARIN'S "BEYOND THE SEA" (7:45 P.M.)
Please invite the crowd up to join us once we get halfway through the tune.

STAGE THREE: FULL-ON PARTY (7:50 P.M.–9:30 P.M.)
Segue straight into songs that will capitalize on the critical mass already on the dance floor.

STAGE FOUR: WINDING DOWN (9:30 P.M.–10:00 P.M.)
Start signaling to the crowd that the evening will be over soon by slowing down the pace of the music.

LAST SONG OF THE NIGHT: PEARL JAM'S "LAST KISS" (10:00 P.M.)
Please announce last call before you play this track.

Deep Breath: It's All Coming Together

By the time you're able to visualize your reception, you're pretty far into the planning process. At this point, your wedding has not only a life of its own but also its own zip code, its own weather patterns, maybe even its own solar system—and you're just a tiny planet in patient orbit, a servant of something much larger than yourself. So go with it. Give in. Rejoice in the positive, and make peace with anything that's not turning out quite the way you planned. And breathe.

P.S. CRAFTILY
EVER AFTER

CHAPTER ELEVEN

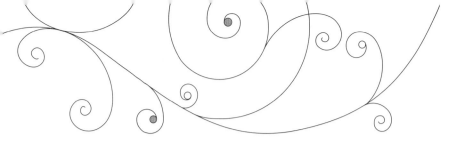

You're still here? Don't you have a wedding to plan? I know, I know, you've got such a full-blown case of wedding fever that you're starting to fear what your life will be like without anything to orchestrate. But here's the truth: After the honeymoon, it's all over but the thank-you notes. And, of course, the photos.

A combination of the two makes the perfect finishing touch to a DIY wedding. Get a picture of the two of you holding handwritten signs, one saying "Thank" and the other saying "You," at a beautiful spot on your honeymoon. Then have them made into cards using a photo-processing Web site. Or, during the reception, get a shot of the two of you with every table and make those pictures into personalized cards. Use them as thank-you notes for gifts, or simply to acknowledge each person or family's presence at your wedding.

Another way to send a more general "thanks for coming" note to your guests is to create an online album of photos capturing a few highlights from the ceremony, reception, and honeymoon. You can then "share" the album via the Web site as you would any other online photo album, typing in a list of addresses and sending a short e-mail that includes a link to your pics. However you do it, I guarantee that people will love to hear from you and be glad to have a visual reminder of the day.

That's the thing about DIY weddings—they're so great that your guests go through withdrawal.

THE DIY GUIDE

DIY Rules Recap

Food, flowers, or finery: a few principles apply to every area of the DIY wedding.

* "Real people," a.k.a. "amateurs," often can do things just as well as "professionals," who, after all, are real people, too.

* Avoid using the word "wedding" when you mention your event to potential vendors. "Party" will suffice—and save you money.

* Word of mouth is the best way to find great people and services.

* If your efforts don't easily turn up the person or service you're looking for, don't kill yourself looking—or settle for something you don't really want—in the name of trying to stay within your extended network. There are plenty of excellent, affordable traditional wedding vendors out there, and there should be at least one willing to customize their services to your specifications.

* If something seems expensive, consider whether the purchase might buy you peace of mind. When you DIY, allow yourself the occasional splurge, for sanity's sake.

* Consider whether you really want to accept a favor. Unless you're working with close friends or family, it's wise to attach a fee to any project, even if it's just a token amount.

* Get everything in writing (unless you have a very close personal relationship that would make such a transaction insulting). See "Contracts 101" on page 214 for more information.

* Bring your guests along. If you do anything unorthodox during your ceremony or reception, be prepared to get on the mic or put up some signage to explain what's happening.

* Delegate until you can't delegate any more. Make sure that you're on duty as little as possible (or not at all!) on your wedding day.

* **Reject the package! Ask for alternatives! Do it your way!**

Contracts 101

You really should try to get everything in writing with each of your vendors, unless you are so close to that person that you're confident it's not necessary. You don't need a full contract—even just jotting down the basic elements of the agreement on a single piece of paper signed by both parties can provide some protection. The Statute of Frauds—which is far from straightforward and has lots of exceptions—basically says that oral contracts are not enforceable for any amount over $500, and they're never enforceable for any exchange of real property. So play it safe and put together a makeshift document.

For example, for a cake order, something like the following, signed by both parties and dated, would be sufficient:

* Three-tier cake, chocolate with vanilla icing

* $500 to be paid when delivered

* To be delivered to Chicago's Drake Hotel at 3 P.M. on Saturday, October 20

With any vendor, just boil down the agreement to its most crucial basics, and get them in writing—how many hours your photographer will shoot, and at what cost, or how many musicians will be in your band, how long they'll play, whether they'll take breaks, and what the cost will be if they exceed the original time frame.

You get the picture. It's easy to do, and, although it doesn't provide the same protection as would a full written agreement laying out specific remedies for "failure to perform," it does provide proof that you had a deal. Plus, should something go awry, having that proof will make it easier for you to recoup your expenses than it would be if you had nothing in writing at all.

Here's another important point: it's always a bad sign if a party refuses to put something in writing. There's no reason someone should be unwilling to sign something as basic as the preceding, and if a vendor refuses, you should proceed with caution.

When should you pursue a more formal contract? It depends on cost, the complexity of the project, and your tolerance for risk. The greater the expense on your end, the more specialized and vendor-specific the endeavor (in other words, how screwed you'd be if they bailed), and the more complex the service they're providing, the more you probably want a full contract. The good news is that your vendors want protection too, and in such situations they're quite likely to have something already worked up. Just read it carefully, make any desired changes in writing, and get every change initialed. Also, make sure to keep all your contracts in a safe place and to keep careful records of any deposits you make—it's not unheard of for vendors to "forget" that they've already pocketed a portion of their fee, and scattered brides and grooms can easily lose track of what they've spent.

In general, always err on the side of caution—when in doubt, seek legal advice!

DIY Team Assignments

Here's a list of the jobs you may want to assign for the Big Day:

Deputy—Someone who stands in for you whenever possible. Should be someone who can be blunt and truthful with you without hurting your feelings.

Paymaster—Someone to hand payments to officiant, musicians, and others.

DJ or iPod attendant—A person who's equipped with extra power cords, and troubleshooting skills.

Runners—People to get drinks and/or food for vendors who will be immobile or very busy during the reception, such as the DJ and photographer.

Flower or decoration maven and minions—The helpers who will transfer any decorations from ceremony space to reception space.

Makeup pal—A gal (or guy!) who can lend an artful eye and hand, from shopping expeditions to trial runs to day-of application and touch-ups.

Photographer's assistant/checklist keeper—Someone to help wrangle equipment, and guests, too—as well as make sure that the photographer captures all the images you'd hate to miss.

Servers—If you're not using a caterer, you'll need enough able bodies to manage whatever food and beverages you're serving. Don't forget that things like ice, clean glassware, and perhaps even the food itself will need replenishing throughout the evening, and that you'll want plenty of people to help clean up.

Barfly—Someone to keep an eye on how the liquor is being served and ensure that you don't run out.

Guest book attendant—One who's handy with a camera, if you're doing a photo guestbook.

General helpers—People who will help assemble invitations, programs, and/or favors in the months and weeks leading up to the wedding.

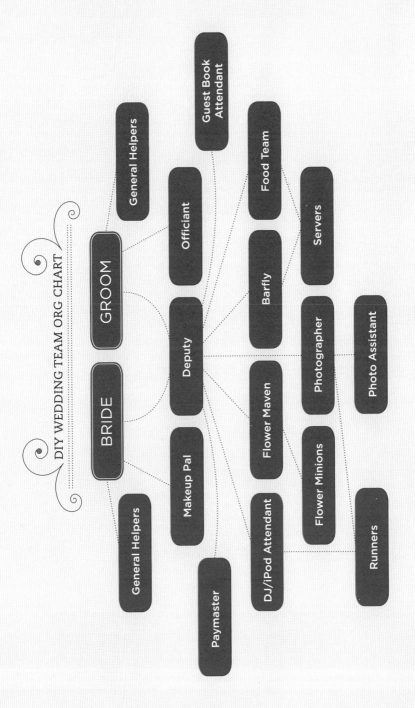

DIY WEDDING TEAM ORG CHART

BRIDE

GROOM

General Helpers

General Helpers

Officiant

Guest Book Attendant

Deputy

Food Team

Makeup Pal

Barfly

Servers

Paymaster

Flower Maven

Photographer

Photo Assistant

DJ/iPod Attendant

Flower Minions

Runners

Resources

Here are more sources for insight, ideas, and expertise, as well as the materials you'll need to bring your DIY dream to life. Although the services provided by most of the listed sites will be self-explanatory, I've included notes in the places where more information might be helpful.

Attire

Dresses and Inspiration

www.antiquedress.com

www.davenportandco.com

www.enokiworld.com

www.indiebride.com/trousseau/index.html (*A well curated marketplace for gently used or unworn dresses offered for sale by their owners.*)

www.retrodress.com

www.thefrock.com

www.vintagegown.com

www.vintagevixen.com

Vintage Boutiques

A few stores worth checking out in person—most great vintage wedding dress boutiques are in big cities, but many such stores also sell online.

Chicago

www.silvermoonvintage.com

Los Angeles

www.paris1900.com

Miami

www.cmadeleines.com

New York

www.adriennesny.com (*A sweet little shop with plenty of off-the-rack beauties that also does custom work, much of it with vintage fabric.*)

www.allanandsuzi.net (*More evening wear than straight-up bridal, but still useful.*)

www.michaelsconsignment.com

Seattle

www.isadoras.com (*Estate jewelry, too!*)

Vintage Patterns

www.avintagewedding.com

www.oldpatterns.com

www.sovintagepatterns.com

Fabric

www.fabrics.net (*Learn about fabric, and get help with your search for a particular kind. Retailers with possible matches in stock will respond to your request and provide samples.*)

Shoes

www.bellissimabridalshoes.com

www.danceshoesonline.com

www.jcrew.com

www.myglassslipper.com

www.showtimedanceshoes.com

Baubles

www.bluemud.com (*Sterling silver charms.*)

www.kinteraarts.com/bead-societies.html (*A directory of "bead societies" across the country.*)

Invitations

Letterpress

www.bellafigura.com

www.briarpress.org *(Community site for letterpress printers. Browse listings or post a "help wanted" ad.)*

www.dsletterpressguide.blogspot.com *(Fab guide to letterpress printers from the design blog design*sponge.)*

www.hellolucky.com

www.howdesign.com/dt/letterpressprinters.pdf *(How magazine's list of letterpress printers across the country.)*

www.paperstudio.com

www.peculiarpairpress.com

Paper and Envelopes

www.jampaper.com

www.katespaperie.com

www.paperpresentation.com

www.paper-source.com

www.wastenotpaper.com *(Wholesale.)*

Design-It-Yourself Invitation Sites

www.aldengrace.com

www.finestationery.com

www.gartnerstudios.com

www.mygatsby.com

www.penandparchment.net

www.timelessinvitations.com

www.youreinvited.net

Customized Stampers and Return Address Stickers

www.customembossers.com
www.rubberstampchamp.com
www.thestampmaker.com

Rubber Stamps

www.addictedtorubberstamps.com
www.gwenfrostic.com
www.impressrubberstamps.com *(custom stamps from any design)*
www.stampusa.com *(ditto)*

Personal Wedding Web Sites

www.ewedding.com
www.mymemorypage.com
www.theknot.com
www.theweddingtracker.com
www.weddingwebsites.com *(comparisons and reviews of other vendors)*
www.weddingwindow.com

Bookshelf

Card Crafting: Over 45 Ideas for Making Greeting Cards and Stationery by Gillian Souter

Creative Greeting Cards by Sandi Genovese

Greeting Cards Made Easy by Susan Penny (editor)

Handmade Greeting Cards by Maureen Crawford

Stenciling & Embossing Greeting Cards: 18 Quick Creative, Unique and Easy-to-Do Projects by Judith Barker

*Also, check the magazine rack at a local bookstore for titles like Paper Crafts, Take Ten, The Stamper's Sampler, Cloth Paper Scissors, *and* Card Creations.

Photos

Processing Sites for Guest Books or Invitations
www.kodakgallery.com
www.photocardcreations.com
www.shutterfly.com
www.snapfish.com

National Photo Booth Rental Source
www.photo-me.com

Polaroid Products
www.i-zone.com
www.polaroid.com

Food and Drink

Recipes and Inspiration
www.chow.com
www.epicurious.com
www.foodnetwork.com
www.webtender.com

Bookshelf
Martha Stewart's Hors d'Oeuvres Handbook by Martha Stewart

Flowers

Educational
www.aboutflowers.com
www.marthastewart.com/living
www.yougrowgirl.com

Wholesale

www.wffsa.org *(Search for a wholesale florist in your area.)*

Web-Based Suppliers

All of the following offer some kind of wedding package, which may or may not be what you're looking for.

www.driedflowers.com *(Branches, berries, moss, pods, etc.)*

www.farmstogo.com

www.fiftyflowers.com

www.flowersales.com

www.freshroses.com

www.growersbox.com

www.onlinewholesaleflowers.com

www.rosesource.com

Organic

www.organicbouquet.com

Bookshelf

The Complete Book of Garlands, Circles and Decorative Wreaths by Terence Moore

The Complete Book of Wreaths by Chris Rankin

Wreaths and Garlands: Home Decorating Workbooks with 20 Step-by-Step Projects by Lisl Dennis

Favors

Candy and Other Treats

www.economycandy.com

www.fortunecookiestore.com *(custom fortune cookies!)*

www.gleegum.com *(all-natural gum plus make-your-own kits)*

www.jellybelly.com

www.mymms.com *(custom M&M's)*
www.saltworks.com *(bath salts)*

Rings

www.doyledoyle.com
www.greenkarat.com
www.randbrand.com *(South African conflict-free diamonds)*

Bookshelf

*Jewelry and Gems, The Buying Guide: How to Buy Diamonds, Pearls,
Colored Gemstones, Gold, and Jewelry with Confidence and Knowledge*
by Antoinette L. Matlins and Antonio C. Bonanno
*Warman's Jewelry: A Fully Illustrated Identification and Price Guide to 18th,
19th and 20th Century Fine and Costume Jewelry (3rd edition)*
by Christie Romero

Ceremony

Wedding Web Casts

www.vowcast.com
www.webcastyourwedding.net
www.yourwebcast.com

Reception

General Inspiration

www.craftzine.com
www.designsponge.blogspot.com

Paper Products, Vases, Containers, and More

www.containerstore.com

www.foryourparty.com

www.orientaltradingcompany.com

www.pearlriver.com

www.save-on-crafts.com

Vinyl Wall Lettering and Stencils

www.stencil-library.com

www.vinylattraction.com

www.wallwords.com

www.whatisblik.com

www.wonderfulgraffiti.com

Candles

www.churchcandlesonline.com

www.discountcandleshop.com

Greener and More Socially Conscious Weddings

www.botanicalpaperworks.com

www.ecoprint.com

www.gaiam.com

www.greenhome.com

www.greenerprinter.com

www.greensage.com

www.idofoundation.org

www.organicweddings.com

www.plantablepaper.com

www.portovert.com

Index

Attire
  bride's, 40–59
  bridesmaids', 66–72
  groom's, 63–65
  guests', 78
  resources for, 218–20
Bar, 118–22
Bartering, 30
Bouquets, 138–42, 186
Boutonnieres, 142, 143
Bride's attire, 40–59
Bridesmaids' attire, 66–72
Budget, 16–20

Cake, 116–18
Candles, 225
Caterers, 109, 114–16
Centerpieces, 144–47
Ceremony
  creating, 175–76, 183–87
  decorations for, 192–93
  location of, 21, 34–35
  music for, 188–89
  officiant for, 175–82
  outline of, 190–91
Colors, 33, 67
Conflicts, 29, 184
Contracts, 214–15
Corsages, 142
Cuff links, 65

Date, setting, 35–36
Decorations, 192–93
Delegating, importance of, 12, 27
DIY rules, 213
DJ, 203–5
Drinks, 118–22, 222

Earrings, 70–72
Environmental considerations, 20–22, 93, 120, 165–66

Favors, 148–61, 224
Flowers, 127–47, 197, 223–24
Food, 109–18, 123–25, 222

Goody bags, 154–56
Graphic designers, 81–82
Groom's attire, 63–65
Guest book, 103, 104, 186, 202, 222
Guests
  attire of, 78
  involving, in ceremony, 185–86
  list of, 34
  thinking of, 196

Hair, 60–62
Handkerchiefs, 68–69
Helpers, 12, 24–29, 216–17

Inspiration, 30–33
Invitations, 75–91, 93, 95, 220–22